I Wanted to Write a Poem

Books by William Carlos Williams

1909 Poems
1913 The Tempers
1917 Al que quiere!
1920 Kora in Hell: Improvisations
1921 Sour Grapes
1923 Spring and All
1923 The Great American Novel
1925 In the American Grain
1928 A Voyage to Pagany
1932 A Novelette and Other Prose
The Knife of the Times
The Cod Head
1934 Collected Poems, 1921-1931
1935 An Early Martyr
1936 Adam and Eve & The City
1937 White Mule
1938 The Complete Collected Poems of William Carlos Williams
Life Along the Passaic River
1940 In the Money
1941 The Broken Span
1944 The Wedge
1946 Paterson, Book I
First Act
1948 Paterson, Book II
A Dream of Love
The Clouds
1949 The Pink Church
Paterson, Book III
1950 A Beginning on the Short Story
Make Light of It: Collected Stories
Collected Later Poems
1951 Paterson, Book IV
Collected Earlier Poems
The Autobiography of William Carlos Williams
1952 The Build-Up
1954 The Desert Music
The Dog and The Fever (Tr. of Quevedo)
Selected Essays
1955 Journey to Love
1957 Selected Letters
1958 I Wanted to Write a Poem
Paterson, Book V
1959 Yes, Mrs. Williams
1961 The Farmers' Daughters (Collected Stories)
Many Loves (Collected Plays)
1962 Pictures from Brueghel
1966 The William Carlos Williams Reader
1970 Imaginations
A Voyage to Pagany
1974 The Embodiment of Knowledge
1976 Interviews with W. C. Williams
1978 A Recognizable Image: WCW on Art and Artists

WILLIAM CARLOS WILLIAMS

I Wanted to Write a Poem

The Autobiography of the Works of a Poet

reported and edited by
Edith Heal

A NEW DIRECTIONS BOOK

Manufactured in the United States of America
Originally published clothbound in 1958 by Beacon Press; revised and reissued in 1967.
First published as New Directions Paperbook 469 in 1978
Published simultaneously in Canada by McClelland & Stewart, Ltd.

Library of Congress Cataloging in Publication Data

Williams, William Carlos, 1883–1963.
I wanted to write a poem.
(A New Directions Book)
1. Williams, William Carlos, 1883–1963—Interviews.
2. Williams, William Carlos, 1883–1963—Bibliography.
I. Berrien, Edith Heal, 1903– II. Title.
PS3545.I544Z52 1978 811'.5'2 78-6645
ISBN 0-8112-0707-2

New Directions Books are published for James Laughlin
by New Directions Publishing Corporation,
333 Sixth Avenue, New York 10014

INTRODUCTION

This little book presents the engaging performance of a poet conversing about his own world of poetry. And because the poet is William Carlos Williams, this world is as freshly and sharply portrayed as the paint on his famous wheelbarrow.

It is an intensely personal history, stormy, tender, bittersweet, and uphill a good deal of the way. It tells of the birth of poetry, his poetry, identified with no literary ancestors, as independent as the American idiom he believes in so passionately.

The door of 9 Ridge Road in Rutherford, New Jersey, is massive, Victorian, and always unlocked. Hundreds of neighbors, former patients, poets, and students ring the bell and walk in as I did one morning in May in the poet's seventy-third year. Would the poet be willing to work with me on a descriptive bibliography of his works including his own account of the writing experience?

"You mean," Dr. Williams said, "the history of the writing itself? Not a biography, except, of course, where biographical material touches the work?"

Yes, this was exactly what I meant; a notebook by recall of a writer in the act of being a writer.

Dr. Williams said, "You're going to make me work."

For five months I met with the poet and his wife, the Bill and Floss you will hear talking in these pages. The interviewer seldom asked a question because the poet did his own searching. I simply took notes. And Floss's acute observations were an important part of these notes.

There was no set plan other than collecting the bibliographical material chronologically from Mrs. Williams' complete collection of published pamphlets and books. As soon as the interviews began I saw that there was far more than the bare bones of bibliographical data waiting for me. The books themselves, with their tantalizing title pages naming publishers unknown to the contemporary 'fifties, promised a nostalgic review of the early twentieth-century literary world. The amazing change in the poetry offered an illuminating study of the poet's lifetime preoccupation with technique: starting with imitations of the classical, bludgeoning into free forms, arriving finally at the theory of the "variable foot," Williams' triumph in combining form and freedom.

The collection as a whole, between forty and fifty works dating from 1909 through 1957, shows William Carlos Williams in the tradition of enduring writers, not only an acknowledged poet of stature but important as essayist, short story writer, playwright, and novelist. It is without exception a serious body of work, the dedication of a man who discovered a vocation and has lived to honor it.

As in many bibliographies, you will find recorded an *Autobiography* which the author cheerfully admits was written with speed, inaccuracy, and gusto. I mention it because certain instances in the *Autobiography* are touched upon in the interviews. But wherever autobiographical facts recur here, they are interpreted from a different point of view. Anything "lived" by William

Carlos Williams in this book is "lived" in terms of his writing.

We decided to work chronologically because we all felt the real value to our readers would be showing them the progressive development of the poet. This meant starting a long way before publication, as far back as a small boy learning his first poem, the prayer his grandmother taught him. All through the hot sleepy summer Floss charted our leisurely course, taking the books from her secretary shelves, one by one, beginning with the extremely rare first book of poems published privately in 1909. Her collection, we believe, is the only complete one in existence. Nearly complete collections for those who wish to examine them are housed at the University of Buffalo, Yale University, and the Rutherford Public Library.

There was an air of discovery about the whole procedure: the poet's excited "Why I'd forgotten this dedication," the unexpected appearance of reviews that had been tucked away in the pages of the books, pencilled corrections in the text, scrawled first drafts on prescription blanks.

We thought about format. Dr. Williams wanted to keep the illusion of talking even though the words had to be inevitably printed. He was pleased when we solved the mechanical problem of getting rid of quotation marks, which he'd always hated anyway. This was done by page division; a larger type face in a second color separates the bibliographical data from the body of the page which is given over to the account of the poet, told in the first person. Interruptions from Floss and me, as well as quoted excerpts, are set apart from the poet's monologue by use of a smaller type face. Paragraphing is accomplished by spacing between paragraphs to give the effect of a burst of speech because that is exactly the way the words came to me.

There was no attempt to include in the bibliography the monumental material published in magazines. However, whenever the role of a particular magazine plays a significant part in his work, Dr. Williams has discussed it.

Although Dr. Williams' story was "talked" and not written, the style seems to me to be close to the vigor of language that is characteristic of all his works. It is perhaps leaner, more quickly paced than if it had come straight from the typewriter. And perhaps the result is unique Williams. I have a feeling it could never have come from the typewriter. The sheer mechanics of searching each book, searching memory at the same time, would surely have proved frustrating to a man whose whole life has been directed to going forward. I feel sure that the clean piece of paper in Dr. Williams' typewriter is always the invitation to create something new.

I hope that the check list will be of use to future bibliographers. I hope even more that Dr. Williams' book will reach students and young poets. It is an amazing story of self-development, showing how an individual poet's style was made, through imitation at first, through dissatisfaction in imitation, and finally in bold pioneering.

I should like to acknowledge my gratitude to Mrs.

Williams, who trusted me with the key to her secretary so that I might examine each book myself. The key is a necessity. The poet is famous for giving away, not only his shirt, but rare first editions. And I am deeply grateful to Lewis Leary, bibliographer and Professor of English at Columbia University, who not only assured me this book should be created but also guided me in the ways of bibliography. A version of the book with more detailed bibliographical material, including contents, physical descriptions, and reviews of the earlier books, can be found in Carpenter Library, Columbia University, catalogued with Essays for the Master's Degree, under the name of Edith Heal Berrien.

I should pay tribute also to Allen Tate's accurate alphabetical check list of the poet's works which I used as a cross reference. It appears in *Sixty American Poets, 1896-1944,* The Library of Congress, Revised Edition, pages 143 through 146, covering the publications of William Carlos Williams through 1954.

EDITH HEAL

Fairleigh Dickinson University
Rutherford, New Jersey

I wanted to write a poem
that you would understand.
For what good is it to me
if you can't understand it?
But you got to try hard—

WILLIAM CARLOS WILLIAMS, from "January Morning"

Was he a born poet, wanting to write as far back as he could remember?

No, no. It began with a heart attack. I was sixteen or seventeen. There was a race. Mismanaged. I ran the eight laps. Someone called, "You've got another lap to run. I ran it. I was sick, vomiting sick, and my head hurt. When I got home my family called old Doc Calhoun. He said, "Heart murmur." Oh, I don't know, I may have had rheumatic fever without knowing it. Anyhow, it meant a complete change in my life. I had lived for sports like any other kid. They let me go to school. But no more baseball. No more running. I didn't mind the running too much . . . there was a boy up the street I never could beat. But the rest. Not being with the others after school. I was forced back on myself. I had to think about myself, look into myself. And I began to read.

In Uncle Billy Abbott's class at Horace Mann we read a book of Robert Louis Stevenson's—a travel book I think it was. There was a young man and an upset canoe and a line that said, "I never let go of that paddle." I was crazy about that line. I'd say it over and over to myself. I wrote a theme about it and Uncle Billy Abbott gave me an A —. The best mark I'd ever had. I was thrilled.

The book referred to was *An Inland Voyage* and the line appears at the end of the chapter, "The Oise in Flood."

Stevenson also appears to have been "crazy about that line"—he repeats it four times: "I still clung to my paddle." "And I still held to my paddle." "But there was my paddle in my hand." And finally, "On my tomb, if ever I have one, I mean to get these words inscribed: 'He clung to his paddle.' "

I don't remember learning any nursery rhymes, but I do remember my grandmother teaching me my prayer. It was:

> Gentle Jesus, meek and mild,
> Look upon a little child
> Pity my simplicity. . . .

—and the rest of it. I can still say it word for word. But at one point I refused to say it every night. I must have been very little. I didn't see why I had to say it every night. I'd say, "I'm not going to say it tonight"—lying, looking up at the ceiling, expecting to be struck dead.

My father was an Englishman who never got over being an Englishman. He had a love of the written word. Shakespeare meant everything to him. He read the plays to mother and my brother and myself. He read well. I was deeply impressed. He read Negro dialect poems, too; simple poetry but it had swing and rhythm and quiet humor. I remember one poem, "Accountability." Paul Lawrence Dunbar wrote it. "Put on de kettle . . . I got one of mastah's chickens"—something like that. And Pop read passages from the Bible, over and over. Isaiah was my favorite. I was not influenced by the New Testament.

I thought the most impressive thing in the church service was the doxology: "The Peace of God which passeth all understanding"—I used to feel that peace when I heard that line. Yet I wasn't really religious. I went to church to hear the readings and the music. But I'm afraid I *was* rather a sanctimonious young man.

My brother Ed who was later to become a distinguished architect was my first intimate. He was a year younger and bigger almost from the start. We grew up cheek and jowl together. It was nip and tuck with us when we found my mother's discarded oil colors in the attic, the old tubes half squeezed out. I remember the cobalt, smaller than the other tubes because it was expensive, and the palette showing heavy use. I might easily have become a painter and in some ways I regret that I did not go on with it except that the articulate art of poetry gave a more immediate opportunity for the attack.

At first, not even my brother knew about my new world of books. I didn't talk about it to anyone. My discovery of poetry began with the classics we read at school: "Il Penseroso," "L'Allegro," "Lycidas," *Comus,* "The Ancient Mariner." My but I was excited. But my friends were my former baseball pals. They wouldn't have understood. So it was entirely my own for a long time. And I can't remember consciously thinking at this stage that I wanted to be a poet.

The first line I ever wrote came out of the blue, with no past.

> A black, black cloud
> flew over the sun
> driven by fierce flying
> rain.

The thrill. The discovery. At once, at the same instant, I said to myself, "Ridiculous, the rain can't drive the clouds." So the critical thing was being born at the same time.

And now my brother was my confessor. I wrote him poems and sent him poems. He was at Massachusetts Institute of Technology studying architecture and I was at the University of Pennsylvania studying medicine. Ed spoke to Arlo Bates, his English professor, about me and arranged a meeting. It was the week end of the Harvard-Penn game (which by the way Penn won and I remember I guessed the exact score in a pool and won the money). This was my Keats period. Everything I wrote was bad Keats. I arrived at Mr. Bates' house with my *Endymion* imitation, a big bulky manuscript I'd been slaving over; I don't even remember the name of it. A butler let me in Mr. Bates' bachelor apartment. He was sitting at a desk, the picture of a distinguished man. There was a step down and I tripped and dropped the manuscript. It rolled all over the floor. Mr. Bates was kind. He perused the sonnets and said, "I see you have been reading Keats." "I don't read anything else but him," I said. He said, "Well, you certainly have paid attention to how the sonnet is constructed. I'll tell you a little story. I myself write poems. When I've finished them to my satisfaction I place them in this drawer and there they remain. You may, I can't tell, develop into a writer, but you have a lot to learn. Maybe in time you'll write some good verse. Go on writing, but don't give up medicine. Writing alone is not an easy occupation for a man to follow." This was a turning point in my life. I didn't give up medicine but there was never a minute's thought of giving up writing.

Before meeting Ezra Pound is like B.C. and A.D. I had already started to write and was putting down my immortal thoughts daily. Little poems, pretty bad poems. Not the ones I showed Mr. Bates. More Whitmanesque than Keats. I had read *Leaves of Grass* and I didn't like most of it, but I was impressed with the opening lines of "Song of Myself." My quick spontaneous poems, as opposed to my studied Keatsian sonnets, were written down in thick, stiff-covered copybooks. I can see them still, bound in marbelized paper. There were eighteen of them, full. I was tremendously impressed with them and kept them above my bed. They looked very serious and important. The point is I had something to show when I met Ezra Pound. He was not impressed. He was impressed with his own poetry; but then, I was impressed with my own poetry, too, so we got along all right.

I don't recall my first meeting with him. Someone had told me there was a poet in the class. But I remember exactly how he looked. No beard, of course, then. He had a beautifully heavy head of blond hair of which he was tremendously proud. Leonine. It was really very beautiful hair, wavy. And he held his head high. I wasn't impressed but I imagine the ladies were. He was not athletic, the opposite of all the boys I'd known. But he wasn't effeminate. As low as they come, as I was also, when we talked together. We talked frankly about sex and the desire for women which we were both agonizing over. We were both too refined to enjoy a woman if we could get her. Which was impossible. We were too timid to dare. We were in agony most of the time. Anyhow we survived with the loss of everything but our heads.

I was a listener. I always kept myself free from anything Pound said. I had my own definite things to say and I was learning how to put them on paper so they looked serious to me. In writing a poem I was consciously copying—not Pound—but Keats.

In 1905 I was engaged in writing an acrostic for Hilda Doolittle's birthday. It was a very elaborate acrostic, not only starting each line with the letters in her name, but starting each word in the line, as far as possible, with the initial letter, as:

> Hark Hilda, heptachordian hymns
> Invoke the year's initial ides
> Like liquid, etc.

Ezra was the official lover, but Hilda was very coy and invited us both to come and see her. Ezra said to me, "Are you trying to cut me out?" I said, "No, I'm not thinking of any woman right now, but I like Hilda very much." Ezra Pound and I were not rivals, either for the girl or for the poetry. We were pals, both writing independently and respecting each other. I was impressed because he was studying literature and I wasn't. I was learning from the page when I had a chance. I knew French which impressed Pound and he thought I knew more Spanish than I did. I never let on. I had had only a partial year of Latin at Horace Mann when the course was discontinued. No Greek. I was supposed to be mechanical and my curriculum didn't call for Greek. I remember casting envious eyes at a boy named Wise who was taking Greek, but I didn't have the initiative to change my curriculum. Yet I was conscious that I was losing something that I might have had.

H.D. was studying Greek by herself when I first met her. She was a freshman at Bryn Mawr, in the same class as Marianne Moore, but I don't think they knew each other more than casually and were not aware that each wanted to become a poet. H.D. used to go walking with me in the woods and fields about Upper Darby. We were both writing poems, too shy to let the other see. But once, after being teased for weeks and with my heart in my mouth, I brought her what I had been intent on when I should have been studying pathology. It was an ode, after Keats I presume, on of all things the skunk cabbage!

She listened incredulously and then burst into a guffaw, catching her breath the way only Hilda could—almost hysterical. I never tried it with her again.

Pound met my mother and father. He liked my father very much. My mother? I suppose he was conscious of her. He allowed her to exist. He argued seriously with my father who was a hard-headed Englishman who spoke right out. When he didn't understand something, he said so. I remember Ezra reading one of his poems about a collection of jewels. "That's all right," my father said, "but what does it mean?" Ezra explained that the jewels were the backs of the books in his bookcase. Pop said, "If you mean that, why don't you say it?" I had a funny feeling about Pound; didn't know what kind of an animal he was. I liked him but I didn't want to be like him.

Pound got me to read *Longinus on the Sublime,* but it meant little to me. The books that influenced me were my own discoveries. I knew *Palgrave's Golden Treasury* by heart, and Shakespeare and the romantic poets I've mentioned. The copybook poems, my secret life, the poems I was writing before I met Pound, were what I can only describe as free verse, formless, after Whitman. It is curious that I was so preoccupied with the studied elegance of Keats on one hand and with the raw vigor of Whitman on the other.

Poems. 1909. Rutherford: Privately printed. 22 pp.

This is a small paper-bound pamphlet containing 26 poems. The frontispiece, designed by Edgar Williams, brother of William Carlos Williams, is an old-fashioned scroll, hand-lettered with the following epigraphs:

Happy melodist forever piping songs forever new.
Keats

So all my best is dressing old words new—
Spending again what is already spent.
Shakespeare

The author used the signature William C. Williams in this first book; all others are signed William Carlos Williams. He explained that he deliberated over this for some time, thought first of using W. C. Williams, realized the William and Williams should stay together, decided on William C. Williams, later felt that he wanted to use his full name.

It is typical of me to want my first book of poems to be called simply *Poems.* And also typical that the first poem is called "Innocense" and the second "Simplicity." I appear to be stating my case right from the beginning. The first line in the first poem reads, "Innocense can never perish." I really believed that then, and I really believe it now. It is something intrinsic in a man. And I still care about simplicity. I have been outspoken all my life, but honestly outspoken. I try to say it straight, whatever is to be said.

The poems are obviously young, obviously bad. I took the only form I knew, rhymed couplets, learned from Milton. The poems should be classified as sonnets, not the Shakespearian sonnet, but the sonnets of Keats and other romantic poets. There is a definite Elizabethan influence; I loved the songs in *As You Like It* and I can see plenty of echoes of them in these early poems. My but I was proud of the fifth line in "Innocense": "of youth himself all rose-yclad"—and what a devil of a time the printer had setting it. Mr. Howell, a Rutherford printer, looked over the script and agreed to do it for around $50. The local journeymen, never having set up anything like it in their lives, must have been completely baffled. When I saw the first copy I nearly fainted. It was full of errors. I still have it, with Pop's corrections all through it and suggestions for changes, most of which I adopted. I took a dozen or so of the revised pamphlet to the local stationery store. The price was 25 cents. About four copies were sold. I gave others away. Mr. Howell wrapped up the remainder for safekeeping, about a hundred copies. They were inadvertently burned ten years later.

Yale University was given a copy of this book by Mr. Howell. Dr. Williams knows of three or four copies in private collections. A recent and continuous search for it by residents of Rutherford for the Rutherford Library Collection has failed to locate a copy.

The Tempers. 1913. London: Elkin Mathews. 32 pp.

This book, the first commercially published one, contains nineteen poems, including "El Romancero," a group of four love songs translated from the Spanish. The dedication is to Carlos Hoheb, a brother of the poet's mother, in the practice of medicine.

Six of the poems were published in 1912, a year before the book appeared, in *The Poetry Review,* Vol. I. No. X, published by the Saint Catherine Press, London. The poems were from "The Birth of Venus—Song"; the individual titles: "Homage," "A Man to a Woman," "An Aftersong," "In San Marco, Veneziu," "The Fool's Song," "Hic Jacet." This is the first magazine publication of the poet. The introductory note by Ezra Pound is included here because it is the first published send-off of the then unpublished Williams.

Introductory Note by Ezra Pound

God forbid that I should introduce Mr. Williams as a cosmic force.

To give sound criticism of a man's work after it is published is so difficult a task that we find it rarely done well, but to criticize a man's work before it is written is a task so very difficult that even I hesitate before the undertaking.

Having said recently that no man now living in America writes anything that is of interest to the serious artist, my position is none the more easy.*

Mr. Williams may write some very good poetry. It is not every one of whom one can say that.

Mr. Williams has eschewed many of the current American vices; I therefore respect him. He has not sold his soul to editors. He has not complied with their niminy-piminy restrictions.

He apparently means what he says. He is not overcrowded with false ornament. He seems to have found his art very difficult and to be possessed of some sort of determination which has carried him through certain impasses, one can only hope that his grit is not yet exhausted.

His cadence is, to my sense, genuine, and his verse is sound as a bell—at least in places (e.g., "Homage," second strophe).

But above all these he has one virtue pre-eminent: he has not the magazine touch.

And for this I welcome him. And when I received the sheaf of his verse six months ago, I was glad. I was more glad than I can rationally explain to a critical English audi-

* Without contradiction of this statement, let me add that I have greatly enjoyed *Songs from Vagabondia* by Mr. Bliss Carman and the late Richard Hovey, certain poems by Mr. Robert Gilbert Welsh, and that, considering the tolerance accorded in England to such authors as Mr. Moyes, Mr. Abercrombie and Mr. Figgis, I think there are a number of American works which might be with safety offered to the island market.

ence. I had found at least one compatriot to whom I could talk without a lexicon; some one who has been through somewhat the same mill that I have been through; some one who has apparently a common aim with me. And I would rather confess to a feeling of companionship than to proceed with analyzing verses which the gentle reader may very well judge for himself. Yet I would mention one beautiful simile from another poem, not here printed, where he speaks of a thousand freshets

> . . . crowded
> Like peasants to a fair
> Clear skinned, wild from seclusion.

Often, as in the following interview, Dr. Williams wanted to talk about poetry in relation to his experience with it at the time before he discussed the specific book at hand.

I wanted to tell you about a very wonderful Sunday School teacher, E. J. Luce of Rutherford, a Williams graduate and our church organist. He played the organ badly and sang in a voice to wake the dead. Ed and I sat in the choir to swell the noise. Sometimes we'd help Mr. Luce pump the organ. The point is E. J. Luce used to read philosophy to his Sunday School class: Plato's *Symposium* and Kant's *Critique of Pure Reason.* It was very impressive to me. I enjoyed it very much. I remember it. Pop had given me a dollar as a reward for reading Darwin's *Descent of Man,* so at eighteen I had been exposed, if lightly, to philosophy and it shows in my early poems. I was interested in discovering about life, I put down daily impressions. Certain poems are very real because I was touched by real things. Look at the titles in the early 1909 book: "Hymn to the Spirit of Fraternal Love"—my but I was high falutin'—"Hymn to Perfection"—I *would* have to write a hymn on perfection. And look at this awful line, I'm ashamed of it: "most needs must flare"—I meant it very definitely but it was no language I spoke or even thought. But it was my idea of what a poem should be. I discovered quite soon that it was not what I wanted, but it was all I could do. I was terribly earnest.

I came to look at poetry from a local viewpoint; I had to find out for myself; I'd had no instruction beyond high school literature. When I was inclined to write poems, I was very definitely an American kid, confident of himself and also independent. From the beginning I felt I was *not* English. If poetry had to be written, I had to do it my own way. It all happened very quickly. Somehow poetry and the female sex were allied in my mind. The beauty of girls seemed the same to me as the beauty of a poem. I knew nothing at all about the sexual approach but I had to do something about it. I did it in the only terms I knew, through poetry.

Very early I began to question whether to rhyme and decided: No. I had to start with rhyme because Keats was my master, but from the first I used rhyme independently. I found I couldn't say what I had to say in rhyme. It got in my way. With Whitman, I decided rhyme belonged to another age; it didn't matter; it was not important at all. You can see the exact spot in the early poems where I quit rhyme. I began to begin lines with lower case letters. I thought it pretentious to begin every line with a capital letter. These two decisions, not to rhyme and to begin lines with lower case letters, were made very early. The decisions lasted all the rest of my life.

Mrs. Williams suggested that he dropped punctuation too. Dr. Williams laughed: "Only because I wasn't very skillful."

The rhythmic unit decided the form of my poetry. When I came to the end of a rhythmic unit (not necessarily a sentence) I ended the line. The rhythmic unit was not measured by capitals at the beginning of a line or periods within the lines. I was trying for something. The rhythmic unit usually came to me in a lyrical outburst. I wanted it to look that way on the page. I didn't go in for long lines because of my nervous nature. I couldn't. The rhythmic pace was the pace of speech, an excited pace because I was excited when I wrote. I was discovering, pressed by some violent mood. The lines were short, *not* studied. Very frequently the first draft was the final draft by the time I reached the third book, *Al Que Quiere!*

There is a big jump from the first book to the poems in *The Tempers.* The lines still begin with capitals in *The Tempers,* and there is rhyming, very definitely, but the rhyme schemes are quite complicated . . . irregular rhyme schemes, yet unitive, carrying from beginning to end. The title poem? Something that typifies me. I have always thought of myself as having a temper; I used to lose my temper violently . . . not any more. I was always either excited or depressed. The poems in this period, short, lyrical, were more or less influenced by my meeting with Pound, but even more by *Palgrave's Golden Treasury*. I was budding, had no real confidence in my power, but I wanted to make a poetry of my own and it began to come.

I was conscious of my mother's influence all through this time of writing, her ordeal as a woman and as a foreigner in this country. I've always held her as a mythical figure, remote from me, detached, looking down on an area in which I happened to live, a fantastic world where she was moving as a more or less pathetic figure. Remote, not only because of her Puerto Rican background, but also because of her bewilderment at life in a small town in New Jersey after her years in Paris where she had been an art student. Her interest in art became my interest in art. I was personifying her, her detachment from the world of Rutherford. She seemed an heroic figure, a poetic ideal. I didn't especially admire her; I was attached to her. I had not yet established any sort of independent spirit.

Ezra found an old copy of lyrical poems, out of Spanish Romantic Literature, and knowing that Spanish was spoken in my home, gave them to me. I think most of them were anonymous, the folklore sort of thing. I began to translate some of them, working on and off for a year, finding it difficult but fascinating. Four short ones appear in *The Tempers.* I've always determined to go back to it someday; Spanish still seems to me synonymous with romantic.

Certain poems in *The Tempers,* or perhaps just certain lines in some of the poems, show that I was beginning to turn away from the romantic. It may have been my studies in medicine; it may have been my intense feeling of Americanism; anyhow I knew that I wanted reality in my poetry and I began to try to let it speak.

It was Ezra Pound who arranged for the publication of *The Tempers.* I paid $50 to Elkin Mathews, the English publisher, and there was a mix-up. For at least five years they kept on billing me for the $50, though the money had been paid. Perhaps they thought I was a rich American.

"No," Mrs. Williams said, "it was absurd but it was probably bad bookkeeping."

My first magazine publication in America appeared in June *Poetry,* 1913. I had sent them a batch of poems which they turned down flat. I was furious. Floss said, "If I were the editor of that magazine *I'd* turn down what *you* sent." So *she* picked a batch and they accepted them *all.*

The poems were "Peace on Earth," p. 93; "Sicilian Emigrant's Song," p. 94; "Postlude," p. 95; "Proof of Immortality," p. 96.

As I have said before, this was a period of finding a poetry of my own. I wanted order, which I appreciated. The orderliness of verse appealed to me—as it must to any man—but even more I wanted a new order. I was positively repelled by the old order which, to me, amounted to restriction.

Al Que Quiere! A Book of Poems. 1917. Boston: The Four Seas Company. 87 pp.

This, the third book, also took $50 out of my pocket. Edmund R. Brown, publisher of the Four Seas Company in Boston, agreed to publish it. No, it was more than $50, but some of the money could be considered toward my fourth book, *Sour Grapes,* which the Four Seas Company also published with no further donation from me.

The figure on the cover was taken from a design on a pebble. To me the design looked like a dancer, and the effect of the dancer was very important—a natural, completely individual pattern. The artist made the outline around the design too geometrical; it should have been irregular, as the pebble was.

My translation of the phrase *Al Que Quiere!* is, "To Him Who Wants It," and I have always associated it with a figure on a soccer field: to him who wants the ball to be passed to him. Moreover I associate it with a particular boy, older than myself, at school with me in 1898 at Château de Lançy near Geneva, Switzerland. He was a fine soccer player and he took me under his wing, got me on the varsity team. His name was Suares, a Spaniard, and as I was half-Spanish, there was a bond. He gave me his school cap when he left, a great honor. The phrase made me think of him, wanting the ball on the soccer field, and of myself. I was convinced nobody in the world of poetry wanted me but I was there willing to pass the ball if anyone did want it.

Around 1914 I began to know other poets. The *Others* movement had started, originated by Walter Arensberg and Alfred Kreymborg. Alfred lived in Grantwood, New Jersey, all year round, in a shack never meant for winter. His wife Gertrude was very devoted and starry-eyed, married to a penniless poet but loving it. Believe me he made her work. I made weekly trips, winter and summer, to help read manuscripts, correct proofs. I finally edited one of the issues and probably paid for it. We published Maxwell Bodenheim. I liked him, felt he needed help; he stayed with Floss and me for awhile. Whenever I wrote at this time, the poems were written with *Others* in mind. I made no attempt to get publication anywhere else; the poems were definitely for *Others.*

Except for the first published poems in the English magazine, *The Poetry Review,* some in another English magazine called *The Egoist,* and the few accepted by *Poetry, Others* got them all and, of course, we—myself and my friends—owned it, so you see I wasn't really cutting much of a figure as a poet.

I met Marianne Moore for the first time in the *Others* days. She had a head of the most glorious auburn hair and eyes—I don't even know to this day whether they were blue or green—but these features were about her only claim to physical beauty. We all loved and not a little feared her not only because of her keen wit but for her skill as a writer of poems. She had a unique style of her own; none of us wanted to copy it but we admired it. Her kindness to *Others* was not without barbs. Her loyalty to the group and to her mother was unflagging. It irritated us somewhat, the mother thing, but there was nothing to do about it.

Until my father's death, I turned to him with my literary problems. We translated a short story from the Spanish together. It was by Rafael Arévalo Martínez, called "El hombre que paraseia un caballo." We had a great argument about the English wording of the title. The literal translation appeared to be "The Man Who Looks Like a Horse," but we weren't satisfied. Finally it came to my father: "The Man Who Resembles a Horse." It was a linguistic triumph which my father and I shared.

I'd like to talk about some of the poems in *Al Que Quiere!* Why did I use the Latin title *Sub Terra* for this poem? I was not pretentious—yes, I guess I was. I thought I was contemptuous of Latin but I suppose I wanted to appear as a Latin scholar which I was not. The idea of the poem is this. I thought of myself as being under the earth, buried in other words, but as any plant is buried, retaining the power to come again. The poem is Spring, the earth giving birth to a new crop of poets, showing that I thought I would some day take my place among them, telling them that I was coming pretty soon. See how earnest and passionate about the idea I was? Look at the last line: "nostrils lipping the wind." Without knowing Greek I had read translations of *The Odes of Theocritus* and felt myself very much attracted by the pastoral mode. But my feeling for the country was not as sophisticated as the pastorals with their picturesque shepherdesses. I was always a country boy, felt myself a country boy. To me the countryside was a real world but nonetheless a poetic world. I have always had a feeling of identity with nature, but not assertive; I have always believed in keeping myself out of the picture. When I spoke of flowers, I *was* a flower, with all the prerogatives of flowers, especially the right to come alive in the Spring.

I was interested in the construction of an image before the image was popular in poetry. The poem "Metric Figure" is an example. I was influenced by my mother's still lifes. I was looking for a metric figure—a new measure. I couldn't find it and I couldn't wait for it. I was too impatient; I had to write.

"Woman Walking"—this is a poem about a poor person, the woman who brought us honey and eggs, a quite different figure from the lovely milkmaids of the pastorals, not at all the Marie Antoinette kind of thing.

"Gulls" is a study in sheer observation, a picture, a quiet poem, as most of the poems in *Al Que Quiere!* are. But it all presaged something. These gulls made a deep impression on me. *Paterson V* must be written, is being written, and the gulls appear at the beginning. Why must it be written? *Paterson IV* ends with the protagonist breaking through the bushes, identifying himself with the land, with America. He finally will die but it can't be categorically stated that death ends *anything*. When you're through with sex, with ambition, what can an old man create? Art, of course, a piece of art that will go beyond him into the lives of young people, the people who haven't had time to create. The old man meets the young people and lives on.

The poems are for the most part short, written in conversational language, as spoken, but rhythmical I think. The stanzas are short; I was searching for some formal arrangement of the lines, perhaps a stanzaic form. I have always had something to say and the sheer sense of what is spoken seemed to me all important, yet I knew the poem must have shape. From this time on you can see the struggle to get a form without deforming the language. In theme, the poems of *Al Que Quiere!* reflect things around me. I was finding out about life. Rather late, I imagine. This was a quiet period, a pre-sex period, although I was married. The "Love Song" addressed to my wife is cryptic, shy. I was trying to tell of the power of love, how it can uproot whole oaks.

"In Harbor," a short nature piece, was praised by Dorothy Pound. She mentioned it in 1913. "M.B." is Maxwell Bodenheim, a theatrical figure to me. "Promenade" is about Billy, my son, when he was first born. I call him "sonny" in the poem.

"El Hombre"—"the man"—is only four short lines. Wallace Stevens wrote a letter praising it and used it as a first verse in one of his own poems. I was deeply touched.

The poem referred to appears as follows in *Harmonium,* by Wallace Stevens.*

Nuances of a Theme by Williams

It's a strange courage
you give me ancient star:

Shine alone in the sunrise
toward which you lend me no part!

* From Wallace Stevens, *The Collected Poems of Wallace Stevens* (New York: Alfred A. Knopf, Inc., 1954).

1

Shine alone, shine nakedly, shine like bronze,
that reflects neither my face nor an inner part
of my being, shine like fire, that mirrors nothing.

2

Lend no part to any humanity that suffuses
you in its own light.
Be not chimera of morning,
Half man, half star.
Be not an intelligence,
Like a widow's bird
Or an old horse.

"Hero" is the military hero, not the romantic hero like Lord Byron. My hero has nothing to do with women in his heroic moments. He is facing danger, death. Female flesh is delicious but at this moment it doesn't concern him.

"Canthara" is Spanish Fly and the legend about it. An old colored man, Mr. Marshall, told me about it, how if you feed it to girls they go crazy and you'll get your desire, an insatiable woman. His description of them exposing all they had to the wind seemed to me an occasion for poetry, so I wrote the poem.

"Mujer"—our wonderful Mother Kitty. We had her twelve years, and when she was ready to die she just went quietly down in the cellar and lay on her side. She was beautiful. So beautiful we decided once to mate her with a thoroughbred. There was a $10 male and a $20 male.

We thought we could afford the $10 male but they called us up and said that Mother Kitty would have nothing to do with him, tore him to pieces. She accepted the $20 male and proceeded to produce just one lone kitten. My what spirit. The last line in the poem will tell you our constant Mother Kitty predicament: "and you return to us in this condition."

"January Morning" appeared in *Others*; Marianne Moore liked it. "Tract" is the one people always ask me to read; I suppose because it has almost a narrative sequence. It's the one that begins:

> I will teach you my townspeople
> how to perform a funeral

The titles of the poems tell you how I looked around me and saw something that suggested a poem: "Man with a Bad Heart," "Child," "The Old Man," "Dedication for a Plot of Ground."

"History" appears to be most impromptu but I worked a lot on it. It is perhaps the first example of a studied poem except for the very early poems which were studied in no uncertain terms when I was trying to imitate Keats. I was self-consciously talking about history and it showed.

The last long poem in *Al Que Quiere!*, "The Wanderer—a Rococo Study," was written before the other poems in the book. Why *Rococo* I don't know except it was one of my mother's favorite words. It is actually a reconstruction from memory of my early Keatsian *Endymion* imitation that I destroyed, burned in a furnace! It is the story of growing up. The old woman in it is my grandmother, raised to heroic proportions. I endowed her with magic qualities. She had seized me from my mother as her special possession, adopted me, and her purpose in life was to make me her own. But my mother ended all that with a terrific slap in the puss.

Kora in Hell: IMPROVISATIONS. 1920. Boston: The Four Seas Company. 86 pp.

Dedication: To Flossie

Reprinted in 1957 by City Lights Books, The Pocket Poets Series, Number Seven, San Francisco, with a new Introduction by the author. 83 pp.

Kora in Hell: IMPROVISATIONS is a unique book, not like any other I have written. It is the one book I have enjoyed referring to more than any of the others. It reveals myself to me and perhaps that is why I have kept it to myself.

The editions of these early books were very small. Only my friends were aware of me. That is perhaps the excuse for telling you about *Kora* in detail.

I had no book in mind when I began the Improvisations.

For a year I used to come home and no matter how late it was before I went to bed I would write *something.* And I kept writing, writing, even if it were only a few words, and at the end of the year there were 365 entries. Even if I had nothing in my mind at all I put something down, and as may be expected, some of the entries were pure nonsense and were rejected when the time for publication came. They were a reflection of the day's happenings more or less, and what I had had to do with them. Some were unintelligible to a stranger and I knew that I would have to interpret them. I was groping around to find a way to include the interpretations when I came upon a book Pound had left in the house, *Varie Poesie* dell' Abate Pietro Metastasio, Venice, 1795. I took the method used by the Abbot of drawing a line to separate my material. First came the Improvisations, those more or less incomprehensible statements, then the dividing line and, in italics, my interpretations of the Improvisations. The book was broken into chapters, headed by Roman numerals; each Improvisation numbered in Arabic. Perhaps, to clarify my description of the format of the book, it will help if I include a page so that you may see exactly how it was set up. I have chosen page 41, one of Floss's favorites. The copy above the line represents my day-by-day notations, off the cuff, thoughts put down like a diary in a year of my life. The remarks below the line are a clarification of the notation.

V

I

Beautiful white corpse of night actually! So the northwest winds of death are mountain sweet after all! All the troubled stars are put to bed now: three bullets from wife's hand none kindlier: in the crown, in the nape and one lower: three starlike holes among a million pocky pores and the moon of your mouth: Venus, Jupiter, Mars, and all the stars melted forthwith into this one good white light over the inquest table,—the traditional moth beating its wings against it—except there are two here. But sweetest are the caresses of the county physician, a little clumsy perhaps—*mais*—! and the Prosecuting Attorney, Peter Valuzzi and the others, waving green arms of maples to the tinkling of the earliest ragpicker's bells. Otherwise—; kindly stupid hands, kindly coarse voices, infinitely soothing, infinitely detached, infinitely beside the question, restfully babbling of how, where, why and night is done and the green edge of yesterday has said all it could.

Remorse is a virtue in that it is a stirrer up of the emotions but it is folly to accept it as a criticism of conduct. So to accept it is to attempt to fit the emotions of a certain state to a preceding state to which they are in no way related. Imagination though it cannot wipe out the sting of remorse can instruct the mind in its proper uses.

The cover design? It represents the ovum in the act of being impregnated, surrounded by spermatozoa, all trying to get in but only one successful. I myself improvised the idea, seeing, symbolically, a design using sperms of various breeds, various races let's say, and directed the artist to vary the shadings of the drawing from white to gray to black. The cell accepts one sperm—that is the beginning of life. I was feeling fresh and I thought it was a beautiful thing and I wanted the world to see it.

The frontispiece? I had seen a drawing by Stuart Davis, a young artist I had never met, which I wanted reproduced in my book because it was as close as possible to my idea of the Improvisations. It was, graphically, exactly what I was trying to do in words, put the Improvisations down as a unit on the page. You must remember I had a strong inclination all my life to be a painter. Under different circumstances I would rather have been a painter than to bother with these god-damn words. I never actually thought of myself as a poet but I knew I had to be an artist in some way. Becoming a poet was the way life arranged it. Anyhow, Floss and I went to Gloucester and got permission from Stuart Davis to use his art—an impressionistic view of the simultaneous.

The book was composed backward. The Improvisations which I have told you about came first; then the Interpretations which appear below the dividing line. Next I arrived at a title and found the Stuart Davis drawing.

I am indebted to Pound for the title. We had talked about Kora, the Greek parallel of Persephone, the legend of Springtime captured and taken to Hades. I thought of myself as Springtime and I felt I was on my way to Hell (but I didn't go very far). This was what the Improvisations were trying to say. I did not bother to include Interpretations for all Improvisations. I used to get very excited; the Interpretations had as much importance to me as the statements.

Finally, when it was all done, I thought of the Prologue which is really an Epilogue. I felt I had to give some indication of myself to the people I knew; sound off, tell the world—especially my intimate friends—how I felt about them. All my gripes to other poets, all my loyalties to other poets, are here in the Prologue. It has been referred to many times because it includes extracts of important letters from people who influenced me in my career. I paid attention very assiduously to what I was told. I often reacted violently, but I weighed what had been told me thoroughly. It was always my *own* mind I was making up. When I was halfway through the Prologue, "Prufrock" appeared. I had a violent feeling that Eliot had betrayed what I believed in. He was looking backward; I was looking forward. He was a conformist, with wit, learning which I did not possess. He knew French, Latin, Arabic, god knows what. I was interested in that. But I felt he had rejected America and I refused to be rejected and so my reaction was violent. I realized the responsibility I must accept. I knew he would influence all subsequent American poets and take them out of my sphere. I had envisaged a new form of poetic composition, a form for the future. It was a shock to me that he was so tremendously successful; my contemporaries flocked to him—away from what I wanted. It forced me to be successful.

Perhaps this wanting to appear more literary than I really was, borrowing from the Greek for my title, and borrowing from the Abbot for the form on the page, was pretentious, but I was proud to be associated with writers of the past.

We turned to the Prologue and I read a page or two aloud. Dr. Williams said shyly: "Perhaps this is the first thing to show me to be a prose writer. As far as can be told, it is the first piece of continuous prose I remember writing." The Prologue, which Dr. Williams feels is significant because it has been quoted and referred to so often, has been reprinted in *Selected Essays,* Random House, 1954.

Sour Grapes. 1921. Boston: The Four Seas Company. 78 pp.

Dedication: To Alfred Kreymborg

The book is dedicated to Alfred Kreymborg. We were intimate friends as I have told you but something happened to change things. I don't know quite how to tell it, but I think it should be told. It may have significance, something to do with the fact that I have never been successful in the theatre. Right at this time (1920 and 21) we were all writing plays, hoping for production in one of the little theatres. I wrote a little play in verse called *The Apple Tree.* I was quite proud of it and sent it to Alfred. He was enthusiastic and told me that it was to be produced with a play of his in a little theatre in New York. But what happened—well, I found out that Alfred was going to have his play produced with Edna St. Vincent Millay's first play, *Aria Da Capo.* I went to Alfred, who said something like this: "Oh well, Bill, we all have to work for ourselves." I said I didn't blame him, that I probably would have done the same thing myself. But I wouldn't have. I asked him to give me back the play. He had lost it. There was only one copy. I remember only two lines from it. Two characters are discussing the sap of the tree. He tastes the sap and says, "It's bitter." She says, "Have some more." It was a sort of dance play, with pantomime between the lines. The apple tree was the mother; the blossoms and fruit were her children. It's all past now but gee it hit me hard. I was so anxious to succeed in the theatre. My first interest was the theatre. I was at home on the stage. I loved to act in college plays. I even contemplated giving up medicine to be a scene-shifter. It was never quite the same with Alfred and me afterward.

The first thing to talk about is the name of the book: *Sour Grapes.* Everyone knows the meaning of sour grapes, but it had a special meaning for me. I've always thought of a poet as *not* a successful man except in his own mind, which is devoted to something entirely different than what the world thinks of as success. The poet puts his soul in his work and if he writes a good poem he *is* successful. When I decided on the title I was playing a game, sticking my fingers up to my nose at the world.

All the poems are poems of disappointment, sorrow. I felt rejected by the world. But secretly I had my own idea. Sour grapes are just as beautiful as any other grapes. The shape, round, perfect, beautiful. I knew it—*my* sour grape —to be just as typical of beauty as *any* grape, sweet or sour. But the world undoubtedly read a sour meaning into my title. I remember one woman, a notorious baroness who lived in a filthy apartment in Greenwich Village. When she saw the title she pounced on it: "You know what that mean—you are a disappointed man"—as if she had made a brilliant discovery.

I was very late, very slow, to find out about the world. This book is all about that sort of thing. The people in the Village could show me so I spent time in the Village. They wanted me to share. I was curious, I'll admit, very curious, but I was having none of it. They wanted me to go to bed just to amuse *them*. I knew that it must be at my own time, in my own place. The real thing is I didn't know *anything* about life. I was completely ignorant. So when the baroness offered to give me syphilis I told her I would rather get it myself without having a *gift* of syphilis.

I used to visit the apartment of Margaret Anderson and Jane Heap, the editors of *The Little Review*. There was a huge swinging bed suspended from the ceiling. We poor males would look timidly at it and marvel.

"I am late with my singing"—the poem "The Late

Singer" begins. I was always conscious of being late. But I was catching up fast with life at this point. People found many of the poems shocking or thought of me as shocking. I was only trying to find the truth, ugly truth as well as beautiful truth. What can a mere man do? I was asked to appear at the Armory Show and I read the poem, "Overture To A Dance of Locomotives." Many of the ladies in the audience left but Mina Loy said it was the best poem read that day. I had a flirtation with Mina—fruitless.

"I don't think you had enough money for Mina," Mrs. Williams said. Dr. Williams laughed. "I remember telling Floss that Mina was asking me the strangest questions about my personal affairs."

The poem called "March" is another studied poem. I submitted it to H.D. (Hilda Doolittle) and her husband Richard Aldington for the second edition of the anthology *Des Imagistes.* They turned it down; they were probably right. It was smart alecky. Hilda wrote me a letter bawling me out. It is used in the Prologue of *Kora in Hell.* She said it's all right to make fun but don't make fun of *yourself.*

This is definitely a mood book, all of it impromptu. When the mood possessed me, I wrote. Whether it was a tree or a woman or a bird, the mood had to be translated into form. To get the line on paper. To make it euphonious. To fit the words so that they went smoothly and still said exactly what I wanted to say. That was what I struggled for. To me, at that time, a poem was an image, the picture was the important thing. As far as I could, with the material I had, I was lyrical, but I was determined to use the material I knew and much of it did not lend itself to lyricism.

"Blizzard" tells about me, the doctor. I had to go out in the snow to make a night call. I can remember the moment the last lines speak of:

> The man turns and there—
> his solitary track stretched out
> upon the world.

"Thursday," "The Dark Day," "Complaint," are all the mood of *Sour Grapes*.

For some reason I included a short prose piece called "The Delicacies"—an impression of beautiful food at a party, image after image piled up, an impression in rhythmic prose.

Straight observation is used in four poems about flowers: "Daisy," "Primrose" (this is the American primrose), "Queen Anne's Lace," "Great Mullen." I thought of them as still lifes. I looked at the actual flowers as they grew. When Whit Burnett asked me to contribute to his anthology, *This Is My Best,* I chose these four poems.

You ask me about the poem "Portrait of the Author." Bob McAlmon, my co-editor on *Contact,* rescued it from the wastebasket. I threw it away because I thought it was sentimental and I was afraid I was imitating Pound. I hated to imitate. But Bob said it was good so I let it survive.

Contact was a "little magazine" edited jointly by Dr. Williams and Robert McAlmon for a few years in the early twenties.

Spring and All. 1923. Dijon: Contact Publishing Co. 93 pp.

Dedication: To Charles Demuth

Have I mentioned the painter Charles Demuth? I met him almost at once when I went down to Penn in my freshman year and we became at once lifelong friends. The men I met in those years I have clung to forever; that's the way I felt about it from the first, that it would be forever, and that's the way it has turned out. With *Spring and All,* it was his turn for a dedication and tribute.

Nobody ever saw it—it had no circulation at all—but I had a lot of fun with it. It consists of poems interspersed with prose, the same idea as IMPROVISATIONS. It was written when all the world was going crazy about typographical form and is really a travesty on the idea. Chapter headings are printed upside down on purpose, the chapters are numbered all out of order, sometimes with a Roman numeral, sometimes with an Arabic, anything that came in handy. The prose is a mixture of philosophy and nonsense. It made sense to me, at least to my disturbed mind—because it *was* disturbed at that time—but I doubt if it made any sense to anyone else.

But the poems were kept pure—no typographical tricks when they appear—set off from the prose. They are numbered consistently; none had titles though they were to have titles later when they were reprinted in *Collected Poems.* Here, for instance, on page 74 are the eight lines later to be known as "The Red Wheelbarrow"—here, without a title, simply a number on a page:

So much depends
upon

a red wheel
barrow

glazed with rain
water

beside the white
chickens

Some of the poems were considered good. "By the road to the contagious hospital" has been praised by the conventional boys for its form.

Pages 1 and 2 of *Spring and All* read to me like a manifesto and seem important enough to quote:

"What do they mean when they say: 'I do not like your poems. Is this what you call poetry? It is the very antithesis of poetry. It is antipoetry. Poetry that used to go hand in hand with life, poetry that interpreted our deepest promptings, poetry that inspired, that led us forward to new discoveries, new depths of tolerance, new heights of exaltation. You moderns! it is the death of poetry that you are accomplishing. No. I cannot understand this work. You have not yet suffered a cruel blow from life. When you have suffered you will write differently. . . .' "

And the poet's answer:

"Perhaps this noble apostrophe means something terrible for me. I am not certain, but for the moment I interpret it to say: 'You have robbed me. God, I am naked. What shall I do?'—By it they mean that when I have suffered (provided I have not done so as yet) I too shall run for cover; that I too shall seek refuge in fantasy. And mind you, I do not say that I will not. To decorate my age."

The Great American Novel. 1923. Paris: Three Mountains Press. 79 pp.

Three hundred copies of this book were printed on Rives hand-made paper.

Physically, this is a beautiful book. William Bird of Paris was responsible for it. It's a travesty on what I considered conventional American writing. People were always talking about the Great American Novel so I thought I'd write it. The heroine is a little Ford car—she was very passionate—a hot little baby. Someday you should read it. You'll have fun.

So I did read it, on a hot summer day when Dr. Williams and his wife were at the seashore. They had given me the keys to the house so that I could look at all the books by myself. Lucy, who has been with the Williams for years, occasionally whisked me upstairs so she could vacuum. Upstairs, like downstairs, is full of books. Dr. Williams' study has an enormous desk with an orderly row of foreign dictionaries and reference books. His typewriter, an electric one, was presented to him by his former colleagues on the staff of the Passaic General Hospital. First, they gave him a dictaphone, but it "frightened him off." I found two passages I should like to quote, neither of them anything to do with the hot little Ford car in love with the truck, which just proved to be incidental fun along the way.

On page 9 of *The Great American Novel,* there are two passages:

If there is progress then there is a novel. Without progress there is nothing. Everything exists from the beginning.

One must begin with words if one is to write. But what then of smell? What then of the hair on the trees or golden brown cherries under the black cliffs?

And on page 66, I found the prose version of what was to become later the poem "The Last Words of My English Grandmother":

But I'll pay you for this, she said as they were sliding her into the ambulance, I'll pay you for this. You young people think you are awfully smart, don't you. I don't want to see them again, those fuzzy things, what are they, trees? Good gracious, do you call this making me comfortable? The two boys had her on the stretcher on the floor. Yes, stay here a week then I can do what I please but you want to do what you please first.

This was published later, in various collections, as:

The Last Words of My English Grandmother

There were some dirty plates
and a glass of milk
beside her on a small table
near the rank, disheveled bed—

Wrinkled and nearly blind
she lay and snored
rousing with anger in her tones
to cry for food,

Gimme something to eat—
They're starving me—
I'm all right—I won't go
to the hospital. No, no, no

Give me something to eat!
Let me take you
to the hospital, I said
and after you are well

you can do as you please.
She smiled, Yes
you do what you please first
then I can do what I please—

Oh, oh, oh! she cried
as the ambulance men lifted
her to the stretcher—
Is this what you call

making me comfortable?
By now her mind was clear—
Oh you think you're smart
you young people,

she said, but I'll tell you
you don't know anything.
Then we started.
On the way

we passed a long row
of elms, she looked at them
awhile out of
the ambulance window and said,

What are all those
fuzzy looking things out there?
Trees? Well, I'm tired
of them and rolled her head away.

Go Go. 1923. Manikin No. 2 (pamphlet). New York: Monroe Wheeler. 22 pp.

Dr. Williams said he remembered nothing about Manikin except that Manikin No. 1 was a collection of Marianne Moore and he was No. 2. Mrs. Williams, looking at the copy of Manikin No. 2, corrected him. The last page carried the announcement of Manikin No. 3, the poems of Marianne

Moore. We speculated on who could have been the poet in Manikin No. 1.

In the American Grain. 1925. New York: Albert & Charles Boni. 235 pp.

Reprinted in 1933. With an introduction by Horace Gregory. New York: New Classics, New Directions. 235 pp.

Reprinted in New Directions Paperbook, No. 53, 1956.

The first chapter in the book, "Eric the Red," was based on a translation of a Norse saga, *The Long Island Book*. Obviously I couldn't imitate the Norse but I chose a style that was barbaric and primitive, as I knew Eric the Red to be. "The Voyage of Columbus" came next. I used the Columbus Journal, and I had a devil of a job making the chapter end with the discovery. Waldo Frank was the only person who recognized the technical difficulty and wrote me a letter praising the ending. I had managed after all kinds of rewriting to tell about the three voyages and at the same time to keep the discovery that occurred in the first voyage for a dramatic ending. It meant turning everything around, ending with the beginning.

The Tenochtitlan chapter was written in big square paragraphs like Inca masonry. I admired the massive walls of fitted masonry—no plaster—just fitted boulders. I took that to be a wonderful example of what I wanted to do with my prose; no patchwork. Marianne Moore admired the conception.

"Ponce de Leon, Fountain of Eternal Youth" is lyrical, extravagant, romantic on purpose. The chapter on De Soto was used by Hart Crane in "The Bridge"—he took what he wanted, why shouldn't he—that's what writing is for.

Chapters from *In the American Grain* appeared as individual essays in *Broom,* An International Magazine, which had a short life but one of great elegance. "Soto and the New World," the piece Dr. Williams felt Hart Crane had been influenced by, appeared in *Broom,* October 1923.

The whole book was written in an excited frame of mind. Floss helped with the research; I was working against time. She is solely responsible for Aaron Burr; she told me what she had read, told it so graphically and vividly I sat down and wrote the whole thing in one sitting. She was satisfied and I was relieved, but I should confess right here that I never read a single book on him!

Charles Boni was interested in the project and encouraged me to go ahead. When I delivered the manuscript to him he said, "What shall we call it?" I stammered around . . . "In the American—" "Grain!" he said and I pounced on it. It was exactly right. We had a lot of fun. When he looked through the manuscript he said, "Are you going to write a book about America without *Lincoln*?" So I wrote a short chapter and he accepted it. He didn't like the chapter on Cotton Mather, thought it was unfair to him. I had spent a lot of time on the witchcraft thing. So he agreed to let it stand. But when the book was published the Boni brothers lost interest in it and quickly remaindered it. I was heartbroken. I used to go up and down Fourth Avenue picking up copies for a dollar to give to my friends.

Glancing at the chapter on Poe, I asked Dr. Williams what his thoughts about Poe were today.

Poe was a poet of his period, a genius but too restricted in his style. He was sold on the classic—couldn't get away from it. He loved the dictionary particularly. His mood captured him; he gave away everything to his mood. The macabre was important to him because he had to break away from the banal world. He had supreme intelligence, mathematical intelligence. He seems to have had a romantic love of women, an idealized love, but he was cut off from the actual touch of female flesh—no reality at all. He existed at the center of his peculiar world. Wasn't able to get away from it; destroyed himself. There is not enough of Sappho for a real comparison but I feel that Poe had the particularization of the image and the perfection of form which we hear about in connection with Sappho. I think he must have been influenced by Racine; he resembles the French poets and seems peculiarly French.

A Voyage to Pagany. 1928. New York: The Macaulay Company. 338 pp.

Dedication: To the first of us all, my old friend Ezra Pound, this book is affectionately dedicated.

A Voyage to Pagany was my first serious novel. The protagonist, Evans, is supposed to have gone on a first trip to Europe alone, an American convinced Europe was turning pagan. He was going there loaded up with Americana—his love of America—to see what was going on in Europe. The protagonist was, of course, myself; his experiences, in a measure, mine. In the actual trip, Floss accompanied me, and the women figures in the story are frequently my conception of my wife. There are other women, imaginary women, women the American might have desired to go to bed with, sometimes a woman whose face had registered in my mind, a woman out of the crowd.

Macaulay saw the manuscript and felt it was too long. I thought "The Venus" was the best chapter in the book so I decided to cut that out and use it separately as a short story. It appeared in the early prose collection *A Novelette and Other Prose,* published in 1932 by TO Publishers. It was reprinted in 1950 in a volume of collected stories, *Make Light of It,* published by Random House.

The story of Venus is based on a romantic experience in Frascati, Italy. Floss and I were fed up with tourists—the noisy English spinsters mostly. We did all our sightseeing by tram, and when the tram arrived we watched to see what destination the spinsters chose, and went in the opposite direction. The Venus herself was a character in a Roman pension who flirted with me even though I was accompanied by my wife. She was young, beautiful. I noticed her. And she noticed me. I described her like this in the story:

> Fraulein von J. seemed very simple, very direct and to his Roman mood miraculously beautiful. In her unstylish long-sleeved German clothes, her rough stockings and heavy walking-shoes, Evans found her, nevertheless, ethereally graceful. But the clear features, the high forehead, the brilliant perfect lips, the well-shaped nose, and best of all the shining mistlike palegold hair unaffectedly drawn back—frightened him. For himself he did not know where to begin. But she looked at him so steadily for some strange reason, as if she recognized him, that he was forced at last to answer her.

A Voyage to Pagany was important to me in my education as a writer. It was told lyrically; the sentences are colorful; much of me as a person—not as a writer—appears. It begins with a sea voyage and a storm. It turned out to be much more romantic than I'd intended but it was fun. My brother made the design for the cover. Today, it is read more attentively than it was when it was first published. There is talk of bringing it out again. It is filled with literary things, descriptions of the opera in Vienna during the Depression, portraits of the aristocrats before the socialists hit them, the *Reitschule*—so much a part of their lives. I hadn't read much of Henry James, but possibly he influenced me. There seems to be a longer flow to the sentences although they are simply constructed. It is a particularly descriptive book; I was copying life as I went along; the trip to the Riviera, on to Vienna, back to Paris, putting it all down, the places I had visited, all romanticized because nobody knew but me what really happened.

A Voyage to Pagany was written in Rutherford in the year 1927 when Mrs. Williams was in Europe with their two sons. She recalls that it was sent to her, chapter by chapter. Dr. Williams said that there was a diary, mostly names and occasions; he did not keep a notebook; the novel is fictionalized recall.

Last Nights of Paris, by Philippe Soupault. Translated from the French by William Carlos Williams, 1929. New York: The Macaulay Company (Transatlantic library). 230 pp.

I had met Soupault in Paris. He was a very amusing person, really amusing, all wound up in Dadaism. I didn't understand what Dadaism was but I liked Soupault. The French edition of his book came out in 1928. I got a copy of it and admired it. It was about a very wonderful little French whore, very intellectual, exotic, strange—one couldn't capture her mood in any way at all—contradictory, amusing. I worked with my mother on the translation. She knew French well and it pleased her to work with me. We worked and worked, intently.

The Cod Head. 1932. San Francisco: Harvest Press. 4 pp.

The Cod Head is a small pamphlet containing the single title poem. Only 125 copies were printed for the friends of *Contempo,* a small magazine of poetry published at Chapel Hill, North Carolina.

A Novelette and Other Prose. (1921-1931). 1932. Toulon: TO Publishers. 126 pp.

TO Publishers, made up of a group of objectivist poets—Louis Zukofsky, Charles Reznikoff, and others—got together and decided to publish some books. *A Novelette and Other Prose* was one of the first to appear. It is quite apparent that I was advancing in the writing of verse much more rapidly than in the writing of prose. I was much more concerned with the writing of verse. The pieces in this book show the influence of Dadaism. I didn't originate Dadaism but I had it in my soul to write it. *Spring and All* shows that. Paris had influenced me;

there is a French feeling in this work. I returned to a more placid style than in *Spring and All* but it was still a tremendous leap ahead of conventional prose. An American reader would have been lost entirely. I had abandoned all hope of getting American readers of a special sort. I wrote for personal satisfaction. This was automatic writing. I sat and faced the paper and wrote. The same method as in the IMPROVISATIONS but the material has advanced; it is more sophisticated.

The Knife of the Times and Other Stories. 1932. ("The Dragon Series," ed. Angel Flores.) Ithaca, N. Y.: The Dragon Press. 164 pp.

Five hundred copies printed.

This is the first book of short stories. The stories are all about people I knew in the town, portraits of people who were my friends. I was impressed by the picture of the times, depression years, the plight of the poor. I felt it very vividly. I felt furious at the country for its lack of progressive ideas. I felt as if I were a radical without being a radical. The plight of the poor in a rich country, I wrote it down as I saw it. The times—that was the knife that was killing them. I was deeply sympathetic and filled with admiration. How amusing they were in spite of their suffering, how gaily they could react to their surroundings. I would have done anything for them, anything but treat them for nothing, and I guess I did that too.

The title story of the book is about a woman living in Rutherford, just beginning to be aware of lesbians. I had bumped into them all my life, but to find a woman telling me about her experience intrigued me. She was not shocked, just amazed. The women remained friends. The lesbian was married and had a family.

In many of the stories I am involved as a physician. I looked plenty, learned plenty; I was still learning about life. We spoke earlier about learning about poetry. In this phase I was learning about life. These people didn't know anything about poetry, anything about literature. They were not interested in me as a writer, but as a man and as a physician. They couldn't do anything but give wholeheartedly of themselves. I wrote it down, without technical tricks. I kept the literary thing to myself. No one knew that I felt the stories might be literary. By the time the next collection of stories came out I had begun to experiment a little. The story "Four Bottles of Beer" from the collection *Life Along the Passaic River* experimented with the paragraph technique, trying to quicken the prose. It is the same technique used in the story I have just finished—one I've been working on for over fifteen years trying to get it right: "The Farmers' Daughters." *The Hudson Review* has accepted it for publication sometime in 1957. The technique comes straight from what I tried to do in "Four Bottles of Beer." "Four Bottles" was not the best story in the collection but I have always felt it was one of the best and Floss thinks it is very funny.

Collected Poems 1921-1931. 1934. Preface by Wallace Stevens. New York: The Objectivist Press. 134 pp.

This is the first volume of collected poems. It contains, besides selections from the ten-year period, a group of poems published prior to 1921: "Della Primavera," "Transportata al Morale," "Spring and All," "The Descent of Winter," "The Flower." "The Red Wheel Barrow"—titled for the first time—makes its first appearance since its original publication in *Spring and All,* where it was one of the numbered poems interspersed with the prose.

The Objectivist Press was the same group who originally called themselves TO. George Oppen, a wealthy young man, was the angel. He wanted to start a publishing house just as some men want to back a play. The Advisory Board consisted of Ezra Pound, Louis Zukofsky, who acted as Secretary, and myself. Others concerned were Carl Rakosi, Charles Reznikoff; we were all contemporaries, pioneers together—or thought we were—dedicated to the idea of publishing the new poetry. The suggestion to collect my poems was a lovely gesture from my own gang and I was deeply moved by it. Louis Zukofsky did most of the work of making the collection. Needless to say, it didn't sell at all. I was pleased when Wallace Stevens agreed to write the Preface but nettled when I read the part where he said I was interested in the anti-poetic. I had never thought consciously of such a thing. As a poet I was using a means of getting an effect. It's all one to me—the anti-poetic is not something to enhance the poetic—it's all one piece. I didn't agree with Stevens that it was a conscious means I was using. I have never been satisfied that the anti-poetic had any validity or even existed.

Mrs. Williams read the passage from the Preface out loud to us and neither she nor I could see anything but high praise in it:

"His passion for the anti-poetic is a blood passion and not a passion of the inkpot. The anti-poetic is his spirit's cure. He needs it as a naked man needs shelter or as an animal needs salt. To a man with a sentimental side the anti-poetic is that truth, that reality to which all of us are forever fleeing."

"I've never understood what upset you about it," Mrs. Williams said. But the Doctor refused to retract; something about the very phrase anti-poetic apparently enraged him as a poet.

We decided to include a few poems published before 1921. One, "Sicilian Emigrant's Song," is a very early poem, different in form from what I was doing when the collection appeared.

I asked Dr. Williams if his poem "Portrait of a Lady" had been suggested by either Henry James or T. S. Eliot. Then I read the poem and we laughed and agreed that it could not possibly have been suggested by the work of either gentlemen. I include it so the reader will see why.

Portrait of a Lady

Your thighs are appletrees
whose blossoms touch the sky.
Which sky? The sky
where Watteau hung a lady's
slipper. Your knees
are a southern breeze—or
a gust of snow. Agh! what
sort of man was Fragonard?
—as if that answered
anything. Ah, yes—below
the knees, since the tune
drops that way, it is
one of those white summer days,
the tall grass of your ankles
flickers upon the shore—
Which shore?
Agh, petals maybe. How
should I know?
Which shore? Which shore?
I said petals from an appletree.

(*The Dial,* August 1920, page 162)

I noticed that the jacket blurb mentioned that Dr. Williams had received two awards up to this time: 1926, The Dial Award for distinguished service to American letters; 1931, The

Guarantor's Prize for poetry awarded by *Poetry: A Magazine of Verse.* He was, of course, pleased?

So pleased I wrote a poem about it: "Lines on Receiving the Dial Award"—it appears in this collection. There was a patient who knew that I liked to collect old bottles—but read about it in the poem.

Lines on Receiving the Dial Award

In the common mind, a corked bottle,
that senate's egg, today the prohibition
we all feel has been a little lifted

The sick carpenter fished up another bottle
empty from his cellar
for me last week, an old ginflask—

What a beauty! a fat quarterflask of
greenish glass, The Father of His Country
embossed upon one side of it
in glass letters capping the green profile
and on the other
A Little more Grape Captain Bragg

A noteworthy antithesis, that, to petty
thievery on a large scale: generous
out of the sand, good to hold and to see—

It approaches poetry and my delight
at having been even for a moment shored
against a degradation
ticked off daily round me like the newspapers

An old empty bottle in my hand
I go through the motions of drinking
drinking to The Dial and its courtesy

An Early Martyr and Other Poems. 1935. New York: The Alcestis Press. 68 pp.

Title page states the poet's age: "aetate suae 52 (in September)." This edition limited to 165 copies. Dedicated to John Coffey.

Perhaps as a carry-over from the slight flare of irritation over the anti-poetic matter in our previous interview, Dr. Williams began his discussion of *An Early Martyr* in a disillusioned mood. "None of them—the poems—had been seen; the magazines wouldn't publish me."

Mrs. Williams said: "Nonsense. *Poetry, The Dial, The Little Review* were all publishing you—I won't have you feeling sorry for yourself."

"But so few poems," Dr. Williams said.

"A poet has a right to write anything he wants," Mrs. Williams said, "but an editor also has a right to decide what he wants to publish. Besides, you weren't the only poet writing and think how few magazines there were and how little space."

Dr. Williams continued to look suitably sad until I read with emphasis the words on the flyleaf: "Many of these poems have been published in the magazines—almost all of them."

We all laughed.

I should tell you about Coffey. He was a young radical who wanted to help the poor, was convinced that they should be helped, and decided to do something about it. He was a poor Irish boy. He had nerve. He decided to steal goods from department stores and succeeded in doing it from Wanamaker's. His idea was to be arrested so that he could make his plea for the poor in court where he would get a lot of publicity. He wrote the police about his successful theft but they refused to let him go to court. Instead they put him in an insane asylum—in for life—but the place got too crowded eventually and they let him go. I identified myself in his defense. No one at that time would have thought of this as communistic—it was simply an unworldly dream and I was sympathetic to the dreamer and the dream. He finally came to realize that no matter how good his idea was, it wouldn't work. The poem "An early martyr" tells about it, the factual details. The title poem is, in effect, a dedication.

Mrs. Williams recalled that *The Freeman* bought the poem, paid for it, but lost their nerve and didn't publish it. This led to a discussion of works sold and *un*published for various reasons.

"We used to laugh," Mrs. Williams said, "at how often Bill appeared in the last issue of a magazine. As soon as they published him, the magazine would blow up."

Adam & Eve & The City. 1936. Peru, Vermont: Alcestis Press. 15-69 pp.

Dedication: To my wife

The book we were examining was one of twenty presentation copies of an edition limited to 167 copies. "Much too beautiful," Mrs. Williams said, and went on to add how strange it was that Bill who always said a book was to be *read* should have been published in such elaborate and expensive editions.

I mentioned that the poems looked beautiful on the page and Dr. Williams explained.

Yes, this was a time when I was working hard for order, searching for a form for the stanzas, making them little units, regular, orderly. The poem "Fine Work with Pitch and Copper" is really telling about my struggle with verse.

The book is a companion piece to *An Early Martyr.* "Adam" and "Eve" are tributes to my father and mother. "Eve" was written first. I wasn't too proud of it. I was rather excited when I wrote it; it had no revision and looked sloppy on the page, but I didn't want to change it; it seemed typically my mother. "Adam," I think, came off better. The poems used the factual material of my parents' lives. "Adam" begins:

He grew up by the sea
on a hot island
inhabited by negroes—mostly.
There he built himself
a boat and a separate room
close to the water
for a piano on which he practiced—
by sheer doggedness
and strength of purpose
striving
like an Englishman
to emulate his Spanish friend
and idol—the weather!

And there he learned
to play the flute—not very well—
Thence he was driven—
out of Paradise—to taste
the death that duty brings
so daintily, so mincingly,
with such a noble air—
that enslaved him all his life
thereafter—

And he left behind
all the curious memories that come
with shells and hurricanes—
the smells
and sounds and glancing looks
that Latins know belong
to boredom and long torrid hours
and Englishmen
will never understand—whom
duty has marked
for special mention—with
a tropic of its own

and its own heavy-winged fowl
and flowers that vomit beauty
at midnight—

The First President. Libretto for an Opera (and Ballet) in Three Acts. 1936. Published in *American Caravan,* a yearbook of American literature, edited by Alfred Kreymborg, Lewis Mumford, and Paul Rosenfeld.

Zorach, William: *Two Drawings.* William Carlos Williams: *Two poems.* 1937. (Pamphlet No. 1.) Stovepipe Press. (8) pp.

Five hundred copies of this pamphlet were printed, for sale at 25 cents a copy.

William Zorach, today a well-known sculptor, and I were together in a play by Alfred Kreymborg produced at the Provincetown Theatre on McDougal Street in the Village —the theatre where Eugene O'Neill's plays were being given. The play was called *Lima Beans.* Zorach was the huckster, Mina Loy and I were the lovers. It ran for several nights. That's all it was: we were theatre pals, and somehow it came about that we combined our work, his two drawings, nudes, and my two poems "Advent of Today" and "The Girl."

White Mule. A Novel. 1937. Norfolk, Conn.: New Directions. 293 pp.

Dedication: To The Kids

After all I was a physician and not only that I was a pediatrician and I'd always wanted to write a book about a baby. I thought I knew what a baby was. So I started to write without too much forethought, the way I always wrote. Writing was very present in my life; I didn't have to build up to the occasion. But what baby should I write about? I'd heard a lot about Flossie's babyhood from her family and I thought it was a good true picture of a baby. Why not write about Floss's babyhood, combining all the material I had learned about her with all that I had learned about babies. I had spent several days a week over a period of three years doing clinical work with babies: a year and a half at the Postgraduate Hospital in New York and a year and a half at the Babies' Hospital. I was filled up with babies and I wanted to write about them. The devil was in me. What should I call the book? Then it came to me: *White Mule.* Floss, I knew, was a mule. And she was white. There was another meaning. At that time, during the Depression, we were drinking White Mule. Floss was like a shot of whiskey to me—her disposition cantankerous, like all wives, riding her man for his own good whether he liked it or not.

The book was written serially and like Dickens I was always just up to the publication deadline. The installments appeared in a magazine called *Pagany* and that's an interesting story. There was a man, Richard Johns in Boston, who was crazy about my novel *A Voyage to Pagany*. He wanted to start a new magazine which he was determined to call *Pagany*. He came to me and asked if I had anything to go in the first issue. I told him I had just started a piece of prose and he said, "Let me publish it." I was all excited, a busy physician never free of any case that might come up but with the incentive of monthly dates of publication. The book had the advantage of the immediate . . . the babies I was seeing every day. I had a lot of fun. I was crazy about babies, the contempt that all babies have for adults. They don't give a damn what goes on and they let go with everything they have and sometimes it's not too attractive. I was saying to myself with every baby I saw, "OK baby—carry on, because I'm going to write you down!" Whatever I'd hear or see at the clinic I'd put in. In particular, I remember one of the mothers telling me how she and her friends took their babies to the gas tanks on the East Side of New York to help cure whooping cough. Naturally the gas didn't cure but there was undoubtedly something in it . . . the whiffs of gas probably brought some kind of relief.

Just at this time James Laughlin appeared, a young Scotchman who was still at Harvard who wanted to start a publishing house. Perhaps he had been reading my story in *Pagany*—I think it must have been that way—anyhow he said what else could he do better than start his publishing with *White Mule*. He was very good to me. I was thrilled to have an actual commercial publisher. The new firm was called New Directions. I was riding high.

The book came out with its white cover. Gee it's a beautiful book. The New York press was crazy about it; all the reviews were favorable and I thought I was *made*. All the lady reviewers were flocking to me. But this is what happened. Mr. Laughlin was also a skier, and right before *White Mule* was published he went to New Zealand as manager of a ski team. He had published only a small quantity of the books which were sold out immediately and there were no more copies available. I got in the car and drove up to Norfolk to see Mr. Laughlin senior. All he said was, "Well, what are *you* going to do about it?" What *could* I do. There were no books and the whole thing blew up. I was heartbroken but there it was—I had to take it.

Life Along the Passaic River. 1938. Norfolk, Conn.: New Directions. 201 pp.

This is a continuation of the stories in *The Knife of the Times.* I was still obsessed by the plight of the poor. The subject matter is the same as that of the earlier stories but I had matured as a writer. I was much freer. I could say what I had to say. The best stories were written at white heat. I would come home from my practice and sit down and write until the story was finished, ten to twelve pages. I seldom revised at all. Most of the stories were published in a magazine called *Blast.* Fred Miller put it out. He lived with his wife and kids in a poor room on the East Side in New York, had no money. I admired him. What he was doing was for art's sake; he wanted nothing for himself, not to make a name. He was dedicated, wanting only to make the new writing heard. I promised to write something for him every week; that was the start of the stories in the volume *Life Along the Passaic River.*

I have never forgotten the stubborn courage of the man, somehow getting together the $25 a month to pay the printer. He has always reminded me of the line in Villon's *Petit Testament* about ink frozen in the inkwell.

The Complete Collected Poems of William Carlos Williams 1906-1938. 1938. Norfolk, Conn.: New Directions. 317 pp.

Placed before me at that time in my life, the year 1938 when I was in the middle fifties, this complete collection of my poetry to date gave me a chance to sit back and appraise not only the poetry but what I had learned about life. Two dominating forces had ruled, were still ruling me: the need to learn all I could about poetry, and the need to learn all I could about life which isn't any more poetry than prose.

This was a period in my life when I was tremendously interested in women. I had never been a roué and women remained an enigma; no two had the same interest for me; they were all different. I was consequently interested in too many of them, and trying to find out about them all. What made them tick? It was a fascinating experimentation. I would draw back from them and try to write it down. When you think of the people dead from the neck up, ossifying life for themselves, not daring to call their lives their own, keeping up a continual lie. Not interested in sex—oh yeah? All I can say is man is only *hors de combat* if he is such a poor specimen he *couldn't* be of interest to *anyone*. I'll die before I've said my fill about women. I feel I am saying flattering things about them but they won't take it. After all there are only two kinds of us, men and women, the he and the she of it, yet some antagonism, some self-defense seems to rise out of a woman when a man tries to understand her. I am so terribly conscious of woman as woman that it is hard for me to write about a woman—I become self-conscious—too aware that she is there ready to tell me I've got her all wrong. But let's talk about poetry!

The *Collected Poems* gave me the whole picture, all I had gone through technically to learn about the making of a poem. I could look at the poems as they lay before me. I could reject the looseness of the free verse. Free verse wasn't verse at all to me. All art is orderly. Yet the early poems disturbed me. They were too conventional, too academic. Still, there was orderliness. My models, Shakespeare, Milton, dated back to a time when men thought in orderly fashion. I felt that modern life had gone beyond that; our poems could not be contained in the strict orderliness of the classics. The greatest problem was that I didn't know how to divide a poem into what perhaps my lyrical sense wanted. Free verse was not the answer. From the beginning I knew that the American language must shape the pattern; later I rejected the word language and spoke of the American idiom—this was a better word than language, less academic, more identified with speech. As I went through the poems I noticed many brief poems, always arranged in couplet or quatrain form. I noticed also that I was peculiarly fascinated by another pattern: the dividing of the little paragraphs in lines of three. I remembered writing several poems as quatrains at first, then in the normal process of concentrating the poem, getting rid of redundancies in the line—and in the attempt to make it go faster—the quatrain changed into a three line stanza, or a five line stanza became a quatrain, as in:

The Nightingales

Original version

My shoes as I lean
unlacing them
stand out upon
flat worsted flowers
under my feet.

Nimbly the shadows
of my fingers play
unlacing
over shoes and flowers.

Revised version

My shoes as I lean
unlacing them
stand out upon
flat worsted flowers.

Nimbly the shadows
of my fingers play
unlacing
over shoes and flowers.

See how much better it conforms to the page, how much better it looks?

In The Money. Part II of *White Mule.* 1940. Norfolk, Conn.: New Directions. 382 pp.

Dedication: To Richard Johns

Both parts, *White Mule* and *In The Money,* were published together by New Directions in 1940, and advertised in 1946 with the title *First Act.*

I asked Dr. Williams about the 1946 title. He said that it was his and that his inflection of the phrase was: *first* act.

This was written as a sequel to *White Mule* but I did not realize until I picked up the book just now that I actually announced on the title page that it was Part II of *White Mule.* Actually the two stories stand alone. The political pitch of this novel is several years later. Floss is still a baby, as mysterious as ever in her own way. It is the story of Flossie's family, specifically the success story of her father and the establishing of his own business in New York as a printer. The facts are true, the situations fictionalized. I hoped it would be a good book but it doesn't come up to *White Mule.* I do not appear in the story; the time sequence takes place long before Floss and I met.

"The baby steals the show," one reviewer said. We read aloud the chapter "Night" with its wonderful interior monologue of the baby, frightened and "touched by the night."

The Broken Span. 1941. ("The Poet of the Month," No. 1.) Norfolk, Conn.: New Directions. 32 pp.

These are poems, some old, some new, appearing in a volume, actually in pamphlet form but rather impressive with its hard cover and cover design, first of a series entitled "The Poet of the Month" which was continued by New Directions for some ten or twelve issues.

One poem should be mentioned, or rather a short stanza, titled:

For the Poem
Paterson

> A man like a city and a woman like a flower—
> who are in love. Two women. Three women.
> Innumerable women, each like a flower. But only
> one man—like a city.

This was used later, arranged somewhat differently, in the early part of *Paterson I.*

Trial Horse No. 1 (Many Loves). An Entertainment in Three Acts and Six Scenes. Published in the *1942 Year Book,* No. 7, New Directions. Pp. 233-305.

A Rutherford group had formed a Little Theatre and Kitty Hoagland asked Dr. Williams to write them some plays. He wrote three, none were produced, and the Little Theatre group ran out of money and disbanded.

The plays were too stiff for Rutherford, not that they were sexy or too modern, just hard to produce. They didn't want to play any of them and didn't, so I was left with three plays on my hands and what to do? I had been to the theatre to see Noel Coward's *Tonight at 8:30*—I thought it was a wonderful idea. I took my own three plays and tried to link them, found a situation I thought took care of all three. The program began with two men on the stage talking about putting on a program of plays. One was the angel of the play, in love with the producer. The other, the producer, was in love with his leading lady, kept secret so the angel wouldn't find out. The plays themselves were unrelated, all taken from my experiences in Rutherford with people I had seen or known. The play was set as a dress rehearsal—that was why the angel was allowed to be present. The script was straight theatre prose, not poetic drama. In the end the angel—or the fairy—turns generous and lets the producer have his leading lady. I still think it's a producible play . . . small theatre groups have tried it and it seems to work.

The Wedge. 1944. Cummington, Mass.: Cummington Press. 109 pp.

Limited to 380 copies.

Dedication: L.Z. (Louis Zukofsky)

The Introduction has been reprinted in *Selected Essays,* Random House, 1954, pages 255-257.

I have always been proud of this book. The Introduction, written in the most forthright prose, is an explanation of my poetic creed at that time—for all time as far as that goes. It was written, as always, in a period of great conviction and excitement. I was convinced I had something to say about poetry.

There is a story connected with this book. I had some new poems and others that had had only magazine publication. Jim Laughlin said he couldn't get any paper —it was wartime. There were two young men living in Cummington, Massachusetts, running the Cummington Press. They were interested in publishing small volumes of poetry. They were very poor, living in a big house that was part of some sort of summer colony. They lived there all year in order to get along. They manned their own press, had a good simple set-up. We met and they decided to do the book for me.

Paterson, Book One. 1946. New York: New Directions.

Book One was included later in successive volumes of the New Classics Series, New Directions, as Parts 2, 3, and 4 were issued.

Author's Note:

This is the first part of a long poem in four parts—that a man in himself is a city, beginning, seeking, achieving and concluding his life in ways which the various aspects of a city may embody—if imaginatively conceived—any city, all the details of which may be made to voice his most intimate convictions. Part One introduces the elemental character of the place. The Second Part will comprise the modern replicas. Three will seek a language to make them vocal, and Four, the river below the falls will be reminiscent of episodes—all that any one man may achieve in a lifetime.

I had known always that I wanted to write a long poem but I didn't know what I wanted to do until I got the idea of a man identified with a city. A man of some intelligence he had to be. Looking around, the idea came to me in a leisurely way. It began before I knew it had begun. I had written a poem called "Paterson" as far back as 1926 which had been singled out for mention by *The Dial* when I received The Dial Award. However, the early poem did not touch on my later theme for the long poem. You have seen, however, that by 1941 the idea was there, expressed in the four lines included in *The Broken Span,* lines that are used word for word, though spaced somewhat differently, in the first few pages of *Paterson I.* I thought, over a period of many years, about the artistic form of the poem. The idea was a metaphysical conception; how to get that into a form probably came gradually.

And the city itself. What city? Like what baby when I decided to write about babies. The problem of the poetics I knew depended upon finding a specific city, one that I knew, so I searched for a city. New York? It couldn't be New York, not anything as big as a metropolis. Rutherford wasn't a city. Passaic wouldn't do. I'd known about Paterson, even written about it as I've mentioned. Suddenly it dawned on me I had a find. I began my investigations. Paterson had a history, an important colonial history. It had, besides, a river—the Passaic, and the Falls. I may have been influenced by James Joyce who had made Dublin the hero of his book. I had been reading *Ulysses.* But I forgot about Joyce and fell in love with my city. The Falls were spectacular; the river was a symbol handed to me. I began to write the beginning, about the stream above the Falls. I read everything I could gather, finding fascinating documentary evidence in a volume published by the Historical Society of Paterson. Here were all the facts I could ask for, details exploited by no one. This was my river and I was going to use it. I had grown up on its banks, seen the filth that polluted it, even dead horses. My early Keats imitation had been a poem about a river.

I took the river as it followed its course down to the sea; all I had to do was follow it and I had a poem. There were the poor who lived on the banks of the river, people I had written about in my stories. And there was the way I felt about life, like a river, following a course. I used documentary prose to break up the poetry, to help shape the form of the poem. Facts about the Indians, about colonial history, celebrated figures of the time appear in very much the same form as they appeared in the documents collected by the Paterson Historical Society.

In my mind, all along, I was disturbed as to how I would put the thing down on the page. Finally I let form take care of itself; the colloquial language, my own language, set the pace. Once in awhile I would worry but I put my worries aside. I wanted to make the thing topical, interesting to the reader. I knew the reader, any reader, would be interested in scandal so scandal went in. The documentary notations were carefully chosen for their live interest, their verisimilitude. Each Part of the poem was planned as a unit complete in itself, reporting the progress of the river.

I called my protagonist Mr. Paterson. When I speak of Paterson throughout the poem, I speak of both the man and the city. Writing continuously for eight years, I brought out each Part as it was completed. There was a great deal of publicity; gratifying things were said. I had thought about it all a long time. I knew I had what I wanted to say. I knew that I wanted to say it in *my* form. I was aware that it wasn't a finished form, yet I knew it was not formless. I had to invent my form, if form it was. I was writing in a modern occidental world; I knew the rules of poetry even though I knew nothing of actual Greek; I respected the rules but I decided I must define the traditional in terms of my own world.

The poem begins with general observations of the conditions of life in the area, "the elemental character of the place" as I said in the Author's Note. A stream has to begin somewhere; that somewhere seemed to me important. The concept of the beginning of a river is of course a symbol of all beginnings.

The Clouds, 1948. Aurora, N.Y., and Cummington, Mass.: Published jointly by the Wells College Press and The Cummington Press. 64 pp.

Limited to 310 numbered copies.

I was in my stride now. I thought I had found my form. I said what I had to say, using the American idiom; I felt free with it. The rhythmical construction of a poem was determined for me by the language as it is spoken. Word of mouth language, not classical English. That feeling of the language was the fountainhead of what I wanted to do. If I could make that distinguished I would have accomplished my purpose. Whatever distinction I succeeded in getting is witnessed by the poems included in *The Clouds.*

The two young men who had brought out *The Wedge* on their hand press were given the opportunity to use the Wells College Press in the making of *The Clouds.*

Floss had kept an undated review from the *New Yorker* which said: "Two fine hand presses have combined forces to produce this beautifully bound and printed limited edition of Dr. Williams's latest lyrics. The poems are as musical, unexpected, and wittily varied as ever."

A Dream of Love. A Play in Three Acts and Eight Scenes. 1948. ("Direction, 6.") New York: New Directions. 107 pp.

This is the version of the play as it was written. The production of "A Dream of Love" was something else again.

"They emasculated it," Mrs. Williams said. "It was not the play Bill wrote."

It didn't run very long—a few nights. All my fellow workers from the Passaic General Hospital brought their wives to see it, said they liked it—one never knows.

The Pink Church. 1949. ("Golden Goose Chapbooks.") Columbus, Ohio: Golden Goose Press.

Dedication: To James Laughlin

I have always been enthusiastic about *The Pink Church* because it expressed my resentment against not necessarily a political situation but a state of affairs. It is a Christian poem, very definitely. The Pink Church stands for the Christian Church. To use the word *pink* as a derogatory term as some people chose to think was absurd and the farthest thing from my mind. I used the word imagistically; the first line of the poem suggests the first pink image: "Pink as dawn in Galilee." The poem goes on to other images. But the contemporary associations with the word *pink* are prejudiced. No doubt it got me into trouble. I was never one to duck trouble if it came to me in a fair way, not a lying way. My conception of Christ as a socialistic figure, related to a generous feeling toward the poor, also confused many. Like Dean Inge of the Church of England I am not at all convinced that communism in its original meaning is any more communistic than Christ's own doctrine. I am obviously not talking about today's meaning of communism and its associations. In the previous book of poems, *The Clouds,* I had included a poem called "Russie" which was also misunderstood.

"Bill was excoriating the Russians," Mrs. Williams said, "but a woman in Washington openly accused him in the press of communistic sentiments."

Yes, excoriating them for their inhuman ways, their brutal and blind ways toward the poor. A poet is used to being misread, but this kind of misreading hurt me deeply. It was just at this time that I received the appointment for the Chair of Poetry at the Library of Congress. I had had a stroke at the time, not a bad one, but crippling for a brief period. Floss wrote them, and they said to take my time. When I was well enough to take care of the duties in Washington—I was anxious to live up to the obligations of this honor—they didn't want me. A release from *The New York Post* Home News of August 4, 1949, more or less tells the story:

A congressional move to reorganize or abolish the fellows of the Library of Congress was revealed today in the continuing controversy over the award of a poetry prize to Ezra Pound . . . Javits (Rep.) pointed out that the Ezra Pound clique among the library fellows has been strengthened by the appointment of William Carlos Williams as a member.

"What the whole mess did was drive Bill into a serious mental depression," Mrs. Williams said. "I am convinced if Bill had gone down as he was able to, he would have been as he is now. Coming after the stroke, it was too much; it set him back tragically, kept him from poetry and communication with the world for years."

It's all in the past now but I should like to say for the record that I have always hated today's version of communism . . . I was approached years ago, before communism was known to have its current frightening connotations, and even then I said this is not for me.

Selected Poems. 1949. Introduction by Randall Jarrell. ("The New Classics Series.") New York: New Directions. 140 pp.

Reprinted in New Directions Paperbook, No. 131, 1963. 140 pp.

Randall Jarrell quotes Dr. Williams in the Introduction (xvi-xvii), giving the poet's own explanation of what a poem is:

"A poem is a small (or large) machine made of words. When I say there's nothing sentimental about a poem I mean that there can be no part, as in any other machine, that is redundant. . . . Its movement is intrinsic, undulant, a physical more than a literary character. Therefore, each speech having its own character, the poetry it engenders will be peculiar to that speech also in its own intrinsic form. The effect is beauty, what in a single object resolves our complex feelings of propriety. . . . When a man makes a poem, makes it, mind you, he takes words as he finds them interrelated about him and composes them—without distortion which would mar their exact significances—into an intense expression of his perceptions and ardors that they may constitute a revelation in the speech that he uses. It isn't what he *says* that counts as a work of art, it's what he makes, with such intensity of perception that it lives with an intrinsic movement of its own to verify its authenticity."

Randall Jarrell is a good poet, a clever man. He is still in his formative stages; he is likely to shift at any time. He admired the first two books of *Paterson,* didn't react at all to Book Four—couldn't take the identification of the filthy river with the perversion of the characters at the close of the fourth section of the poem. It was typical of him that he lost track of the poem as a poem and became identified with the characters. I was getting up closer to the city, approaching the mouth of the river, identified with the mouth of the Hudson . . . the Passaic enters into Newark Bay. If you are going to write realistically of the conception of the filth in the world, it can't be pretty. What goes on with people isn't pretty. With the approach to the city, international character began to enter the innocent river and pervert it; sexual perversions, such things that every metropolis when you get to know it houses. Certain human elements can't take the gaff, have to become perverts to satisfy certain longings. When human beings herd together, have to face each other, they are very likely to go crooked. What in the world is an artist to do? He is not a moralist. He *sees* things, reacts to them, must take them into consideration. Therefore when the river reaches pollution, which my river comes to face in Book Four, I had to take the characters and show them graphically. My critics, Randall Jarrell among them—and Marianne Moore had the same reaction—felt that Book Four was less expert than the earlier parts of the poem. It was not as acceptable to them, I believe, because the material I was dealing with was not perceptive. But the poem in Book Four is the same poem as it was in Book One. To have a moral reaction to this section of the poem because I have seen what I have seen is just too bad. Marianne Moore has always been very outspoken in her criticisms of me in private letters. Technically, she doesn't see eye to eye with me. She's a splendid poet in her own right. Randall Jarrell is making his way in the world.

Paterson, Book Two. 1948. New York: New Directions.

Paterson II is a milestone for me. One of the most successful things in it is a passage in section three of the poem which brought about—without realizing it at the time of writing—my final conception of what my own poetry should be; a passage which, sometime later, brought all my thinking about free verse to a head. I think it should be included here so that you can see the pattern.

The descent beckons
                    as the ascent beckoned
                              Memory is a kind

of accomplishment
a sort of renewal
even
an initiation, since the spaces it opens are new
places
inhabited by hordes
heretofore unrealized,

of new kinds—
since their movements
are towards new objectives
(even though formerly they were abandoned)

No defeat is made up entirely of defeat—since
the world it opens is always a place
formerly
unsuspected. A

world lost,
a world unsuspected
beckons to new places
and no whiteness (lost) is so white as the memory
of whiteness

With evening, love wakens
though its shadows
which are alive by reason
of the sun shining—
grow sleepy now and drop away
from desire

Love without shadows stirs now
beginning to waken
as night

advances.

The descent
made up of despairs
and without accomplishment
realizes a new awakening :
which is a reversal
of despair.

For what we cannot accomplish, what
is denied to love,
what we have lost in the anticipation—
a descent follows,
endless and indestructible

Several years afterward in looking over the thing I realized I had hit upon a device (that is the practical focus of a device) which I could not name when I wrote it. My dissatisfaction with free verse came to a head in that I always wanted a verse that was ordered, so it came to me that the concept of the foot itself would have to be altered in our new relativistic world. It took me several years to get the concept clear. I had a feeling that there was somewhere an exact way to define it; the task was to find the word to describe it, to give it an epitaph, and I finally hit upon it. The foot not being fixed is only to be described as variable. If the foot itself is variable it allows order in so-called free verse. Thus the verse becomes not free at all but just simply variable, as all things in life properly are. From the time I hit on this I knew what I was going to have to do.

I have told you before that my two leading forces were trying to know life and trying to find a technique of verse. Now I had it—a sea change. The verse must be coldly, intellectually considered. Not the emotion, the heat of life dominating, but the intellectual concept of the thing itself.

Paterson, Book Three. 1949. New York: New Directions.

Dr. Williams said very little about this volume, explaining, however, that he visited as far as possible every place in Paterson mentioned in the poem. "Book Three tells about the library. I even smelled the library. I hated it."

A Beginning on the Short Story. Notes. 1950. ("The Outcast Chapbooks," No. XVII.) Yonkers, N.Y.: The Alicat Bookshop Press. 23 pp.

Foreword: "The following is the substance of an address delivered in the fall of 1950 to students of the University of Washington, in Seattle, by Dr. Williams."

Dr. Williams showed me a drastically penciled copy that he had done in preparation for the republication of the essay in the *Selected Essays* which Random House published in 1954. "I certainly revised," he said. Mrs. Williams smiled: "It probably needed it."

The Collected Later Poems. 1950. New York: New Directions. 240 pp.

Reprinted in 1963. New York: New Directions. 276 pp.

Make Light of It. Collected Stories. 1950. New York: Random House. 342 pp.

Dedication: For our troops in Korea

The story "Lena" in Part III had never appeared in print. Dr. Williams had finished it shortly before Random House arranged for the collected stories. I had borrowed his only copy to show to a magazine editor in New York. A special delivery letter arrived at my house saying: "Send Lena back quick. She has to be dressed up for a party." The party, of course, was the good news that Random House was publishing the stories.

Whenever I have chosen a title it has interested me to find one with more than one meaning. You remember my explanation of *First Act. Make Light of It* followed the disheartening Library of Congress affair, could be saying, make light of the whole thing, or perhaps: make *light* of it.

The Collected Earlier Poems. 1951. New York: New Directions. 467 pp.

Reprinted in 1954. New York: New Directions. 482 pp.

A companion volume to *The Collected Later Poems.*

Paterson, Book Four. 1951. New York: New Directions.

Autobiography. 1951. New York: Random House. 402 pp.

Reprinted in 1967. New York: New Directions. 413 pp. Also New Directions Paperbook No. 131.

Dedication: To F.H.W.

With my sweet wife's consent I did not let her see this book until it was published.

"Which was a mistake," both Mrs. Williams and many of his friends told him.

I decided if I was going to give an account of my feelings I wasn't going to let people tell me what to feel. If Flossie had seen it, the book never would have been written at all. I trusted to memory about too many things. I didn't make up any of it but I didn't edit—where in some cases I should have. There are also some inaccuracies about dates, places. The book made a lot of people mad. But it was good therapy for me. It got me back to the typewriter in high spirits.

The Build-Up. A Novel. 1952. New York: Random House. 335 pp.

Dedication: For David McDowell

A new publisher entered my life and I was pleased. I had known David McDowell casually when he was with New Directions. He joined Random House and became my editor, negotiating a contract for three books of prose: the first to be a collection of my short stories, *Make Light of It*; the second, the *Autobiography*; and the third, a novel. This was quite an order for a man in my position. I was in my late sixties. I was always impatient. I knew when I signed the contract I had my work cut out for me. The gathering of the short stories was easy and pleasant. Most of the stories had been out of print for years. The *Autobiography* came next. I sat down and wrote it.

"Rapidly and carelessly," Mrs. Williams said, and we all laughed.

And now it was time for the novel. When I wrote *White Mule* and *In The Money* I knew that I had enough material in Floss's family for possibly two more novels.

The Build-Up showed the family at a later period. The texture of the novel was concerned with data of the town where the family lived, which was, of course, my own town, Rutherford. I had trouble. I found much of what I was writing was too personal. I had to change names, fictionalize situations, so that living persons would be protected. As in the case of the *Autobiography,* I was still in a hurry because I had the respect of any businessman for a contract.

Someone had said to me that the only way to make a book seem natural was to write it longhand. I decided to try it. This was not my regular method of writing; I had always composed on the typewriter. I had a very devoted friend and patient, an educated woman, who took the manuscript as I wrote it—at tremendous speed—and transposed my sometimes illegible writing to the neatly typed page. No wonder the book didn't come off. I was interested in the material but I had to be careful about living people. I was awkward in using the longhand method. And very possibly the results were sometimes distorted because of illegible writing transcribed by a second party.

Perhaps the most interesting character in the story was based on my mother-in-law, a striking person, a Norwegian—a Viking as she said. She prided herself on knowing five hundred years of her family history on both sides. This woman, my mother-in-law, had the dominating freshness of Eric the Red and always appealed to me as closely related to Eric the Red. Floss reminds me that she perhaps was related as her mother's name was Ericson. She was not an easy character; wouldn't allow you to say anything in her presence she didn't approve of; but you couldn't forget her.

The Desert Music and Other Poems. 1954. New York: Random House. 90 pp.

Dedication: To Bill and Paul (Dr. Williams' sons)

There is something special about this book. Just before I had my cerebral accident, I had received an invitation to read a poem at Phi Beta Kappa exercises at Harvard. I had no poem to read them so I wrote one. I had just returned from a trip to the West and the picture of the desert country around El Paso was fresh in my mind. I'd crossed the desert and *seen* the desert. It is always important to me to be familiar with what I am writing about. I was honored by the invitation to read at Harvard (but was perhaps not so honored after I had read). The students were tickled to death but some of the gentlemen sitting on the platform disapproved. After all, it is a pretty shocking poem, speaking as it does of the whores of Juarez.

When I recovered from the cerebral attack, I began to write again. My whole interest in poetry now was in developing the concept I had discovered—the variable foot—based on the model of the poem in *Paterson* Book Two, section three. Now, consciously, I knew what I wanted to do. I had a group of poems ready and Dave McDowell said, "You also have the one you did for Harvard—that will make a book." The other poems in *Desert Music* are more important than the title poem because they consciously use what I had discovered.

Selected Essays. 1954. New York: Random House. 342 pp.

Dedication: To the memory of "Uncle" Billy Abbott, the first English teacher who ever gave me an A

This book made me happy because it brought back into print some of the prose that I felt was significant in my development as a writer—the Prologue to *Kora in Hell,* for example, written in 1920 and seen by few other than my friends. I have mentioned in my account of *Kora in Hell* how often I myself have referred to the Prologue throughout the years. The followers of modern poetry may find the letter from Wallace Stevens interesting, and may disagree with my sentiments about T. S. Eliot.

"Comment," the second piece I included in the book, is an answer to the criticisms of the first issue of *Contact.*

Contact was the magazine—a little one of course—that I was concerned with in 1921. We, or rather I, speaking for all of us, defended the first issue with this comment:

We, *Contact,* aim to emphasize the local phase of the game of writing. We realize that it is emphasis only which is our business. We want to give all our energy to the setting up of new vigors of artistic perception, invention and expression in the United States. Only by slow growth, consciously fostered to the point of enthusiasm, will American work of the quality of Marianne Moore's best poetry come to the fore of intelligent attention and the ignorance which has made America an artistic desert be somewhat dissipated. We lack interchange of ideas in our country more than we lack foreign precept. Every effort should be made, we feel, to develop among our serious writers a sense of mutual contact first of all. To this also we are devoted.

The other piece that I feel is important is the Introduction to *The Wedge,* 1944. I think it says what I feel I have learned about the writing of my kind of poetry.

A Dog and the Fever. A Perambulatory Novella by Don Francisco de Quevedo, who published under the name of Pedro Espinosa. Translated by William Carlos Williams and Raquel Hélène Williams, 1954. Hamden, Conn.: The Shoe String Press. 96 pp.

This book, another one that Ezra Pound dropped into the house, offered a challenge to my mother and myself.

She was almost blind when we began to translate it. We'd work out a few phrases, a couple of lines, fight over them, and finally compromise. It was a funny and very scandalous book. Quevedo wrote frankly. Sometimes we were absolutely defeated. We appealed finally to a Professor of Spanish at Johns Hopkins and he simply sent the book back, telling us it was in "15th century Madrid slang" that was impossible to translate. The story appears to be an attack on a member of the church hierarchy in Madrid, implying that some church dignitary had been implicated in the seduction of a girl. To tell that story, to have it accepted by a Spanish-Catholic audience, Quevedo had to write cryptically—you can imagine the problem this was to the translator. Finally we succeeded in getting a translation. It lay there for years. Norman Pearson came to me in 1954, telling me about a group of men at Yale who had more or less sponsored a small offset printing firm. There was an opening for a book. Did I have anything? I fished out the Quevedo thing. It wasn't quite long enough. "Can't you add an Introduction?" Pearson said. I looked through papers written twenty years ago and found an Introduction I'd started, stopped in the middle of a sentence. It needed more, so I wrote it. And the book, to be a book, still needed more. I had also found a piece about my mother, her childhood, so I made it into the true story of our work together on the translation. I was interested in this, didn't care anything about style. Perhaps this is the way to do certain things. Ezra Pound was tickled, thought it was the best piece of prose I'd ever written.

Few people saw the book. But somehow I wasn't sad. It was a very special book, in the tradition of my early ones.

Journey to Love. 1955. New York: Random House. 87 pp.

Dedication: For My Wife

My theory of the variable foot is explicit in the whole thing. I'm convinced it's a valid concept. It may not be for everyone, but it is a way of escaping the formlessness of free verse. The one poem "Asphodel, that greeny flower" has been noticed and enjoyed by many people. The reviews of the book made me very happy.

Sappho. A translation of one of the two existing complete poems by Sappho. 1957. Published in folio by *Poems In Folio,* San Francisco.

My purpose was to speak as I thought this remarkable woman meant to speak—not what the classic English students had done to her in their stilted translations. I had the poem read aloud to me, over and over, in the original Greek by scholars who knew how the words should sound so that I might catch the rise and fall of the beat.

The Lost Poems of William Carlos Williams or The Past Recaptured. 1957. Collected by John C. Thirlwall. (In "New Directions 16," pp. 3-45.) New York: New Directions.

These are sixty-one poems rescued from unpublished sources and out-of-print "little magazines." "I was amazed at what I saw," Dr. Williams said. "It came to me as if it was new work that I had never seen before."

The Selected Letters of William Carlos Williams. 1957. Edited with an Introduction by John C. Thirlwall. New York: McDowell, Obolensky, Inc. 347 pp.

The Farmers' Daughters. A Long Short Story. 1957. *The Hudson Review,* Vol. 10, No. 3 (Autumn Issue).

From My Notes About My Mother. Excerpts from a book in progress. 1957. *The Literary Review,* Fairleigh Dickinson University, Vol. I, No. I (a special William Carlos Williams Issue).

I asked Dr. Williams for a summing up . . . the encouraging things for a poet in the making, his own experience, which he quickly said would parallel the experience of tomorrow's new poet.

The "little magazines" were there, always there, anxious for new material, and I was always anxious to give it to them. They would ask—there was always a new one; still is—and I was always happy to be printed by them. Wonderful things came out of this kind of association, *The Pink Church* for instance. The *Golden Goose* was just another "little magazine." The editors came to me and wanted to do something special; they put out the special volume for me, "The Pink Church" and other poems. Later they published some letters of mine. The whole history of first publication for me lies in the archives of various "little magazines." I love them. I am grateful to them. I shall always support them.

And next, the colleges and universities who have graciously invited me to read my poetry. A reading trip to the West in 1955 took me as far as Seattle with a stop at Washington University, St. Louis, and later readings up and down the Coast. At Wellesley, once, they practically carried me off on their shoulders. I was speechless. You could hear a pin drop. A million girls were there . . . at least it looked that way. A bell kept ringing, it finally stopped. Floss had asked me to read the Coda to "Asphodel" . . . I thought I didn't have time . . . but they stood on their heels and yelled . . . the girls . . .

my god I was breathless, but I said do you really want more and they said yes so I read what Floss knew they would like. They were so adorable. I could have raped them all!

At the University of Chicago, to my astonishment, the reading was to be held in the chapel . . . a chapel that is as big as a cathedral. I stood ("You sat," Floss said) right in the middle of the altar. I read two poems. There was dead silence when I stopped. I finally yelled, "Is there any law against *applauding?*"

Mrs. Williams said, "I was sitting next to the head of the English Department and Mrs. Stevenson, a sponsor of *Poetry* Magazine. I thought, "gosh, what's going to happen?" Mrs. Stevenson said, "Good, it's about time somebody broke that down."

And the people who have cared about collecting what I have done. In the late thirties, Charles Abbott, Librarian of the University of Buffalo, an ex-Rhodes scholar, the originator of the idea of collecting the manuscripts of living poets, came to me and asked if I could give him anything for the permanent collection of original manuscripts of poets which the University of Buffalo was collecting. A very exciting moment for me—nobody had ever offered to "house" me. I turned out my grandmother's metal trunk (the only fireproof thing we had in the house), gave him everything he wanted, including some interesting early editions of Pound, H.D., and their letters, as well as mine. Much later, Yale became interested. Norman Pearson came to see me. Through his interest and influence he secured for me an agreement with Yale for future manuscripts.

And tributes, the wonderful kind that never get into print. Believe it or not, there was once a literary society called *Les Amis de William Carlos Williams.* Founded by no other than Ford Madox Ford, whom I had met in Paris in 1922 at a gay party in his studio for a gang of characters including lesbians and homos, properly introducing me to the international set of the times. I'll never forget big bulky Ford, our host, buzzing awkwardly about the room seeming not to know what to do with himself. For some inscrutable reason, the Englishman trained at Oxford and the country squire who knew all the names decided to become my friend. For ten or twenty years he turned up on my track whenever I thought he had befriended me for the last time. I tremendously admired the Tietjen novels, and that may have had something to do with it. Toward the end of his life, after he had foresworn his allegiance to the Crown of England and become an American citizen, he had the idea of founding a literary society called *Les Amis de William Carlos Williams* after the Parisian fashion. But it should, I always thought, have been called *Les Amis de Ford Madox Ford* . . . for few of the members and practically none of my countrymen knew anything about me. Nevertheless I felt obliged to behave according to the role I was assigned to play, so I did my best, but I was not comfortable in it.

There are younger poets I am interested in. They date back. Robert Lowell, seen for the first time some fifteen years ago, a much younger man than me, appealed to me. His illustrious name of course struck me at once, but I was not affected by that. His style should have been repugnant to me—but it wasn't. The American virus was in his veins. But his rhymed couplets, incongruous as they seemed, had a naive quality about them that attracted me. You couldn't call them or him English. Apart from the subject of the poems, all about New England sailors, American primitives, the Indians and their complex fate, the line he uses is certainly not Pope. I was intrigued and have been eager to follow whatever he writes.

Among the younger poets, I should like to pay tribute to Irving Layton, who seems to me the most accomplished writer of verse in Canada who has come to my attention in the past year. And Tram Combs, honored by the Yale Younger Poets, seems to me to be aware of one of the techniques of modern verse, influenced, I think, by the French.

You confront me with David Dempsey's review of the record album "Pleasure Dome" in the *New York Times* (Nov. 25, 1949), and I find it hard to agree with him.

Williams, who is a baby doctor when he isn't writing poetry, showed the best form. When the needle slid into the final groove he was sewing up his last metaphor. "Sort of like giving birth," he said. "Sound-proof room, red light and a poem you've labored over for days. . . .

I don't think I have read successfully for recordings. I was always self-conscious and too fast and without expression—just to get the thing done. I have never had any proper instruction in stage appearance. I feel that very few people read poetry well unless they have read Shakespeare and are trained actors.

It took a stroke to slow me up . . . finally I was almost incapable of reading, I had to read so carefully. In fact I had to learn to read—took instruction in reading from Hilda Yoder in New York, a specialist in correcting speech defects and public speaking. Twice a week for two months we went through the drill and it gave me confidence. Floss still feels my platform performances are better than my recordings, and she's probably right because I have always responded to a live audience.

And finally, my own town, Rutherford. My interviewer, Edith Heal, has drafted me as judge in a Creative Writing Contest at Fairleigh Dickinson University for the past four years, and it has been exhilarating to see the beginners beginning.

And, graciously, a group of people in my town have collected me. This is a rare and wonderful kind of thing. Under the anonymous title Friends of the Library a collection has been assembled, complete—except for a very few early books, which shall probably be found. I understand there are also shoe boxes filled with reviews, newspaper items, and many rare and elusive magazine publications of the past. There are also photographs and letters, all to be housed, I am told, in a special room which the library is planning to build, designed by my brother, Edgar Williams. Floss and I have helped with the collection but the Friends of the Library have been insistent that we keep our own complete collection intact. All they have asked from us is data on titles, and with the help of the town librarians they have done a magnificent job in tracking me down.

William Carlos Williams died on March 4, 1963. Two months later, the poet was posthumously awarded the Pulitzer Prize in Poetry.

Paterson, Book Five. 1958. New York: New Directions. Also New Directions Paperbook No. 152.

Yes, Mrs. Williams. 1959. New York: McDowell-Obolensky. 143 pp.

Many Loves and Other Plays. 1961. New York: New Directions. 437 pp. Also New Directions Paperbook No. 191. 437 pp.

The Farmers' Daughters. 1961. New York: New Directions. 374 pp. Also New Directions Paperbook No. 106. 374 pp.

Pictures from Brueghel and Other Poems. 1962. New Directions Paperbook No. 118. 184 pp.

The William Carlos Williams Reader. Edited with an Introduction by M. L. Rosenthal. 1966. New York: New Directions. 412 pp.